The Art Of Francis Gonn

ISBN-13: 978-1502391285
ISBN-10: 1502391287

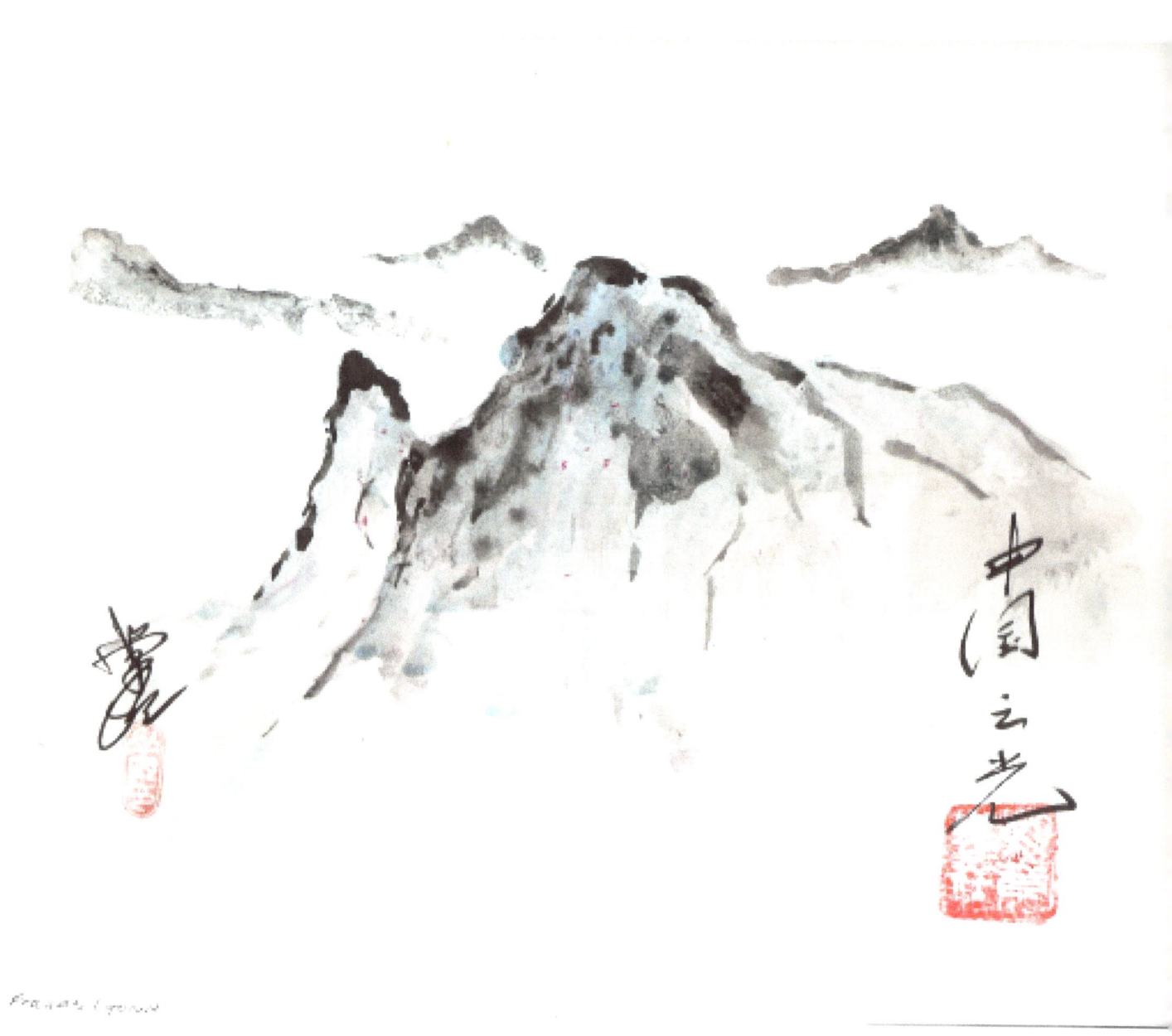

There is an old Chinese Proverbs that stated, a picture is worth a thousand words…
so here are many thousand words.

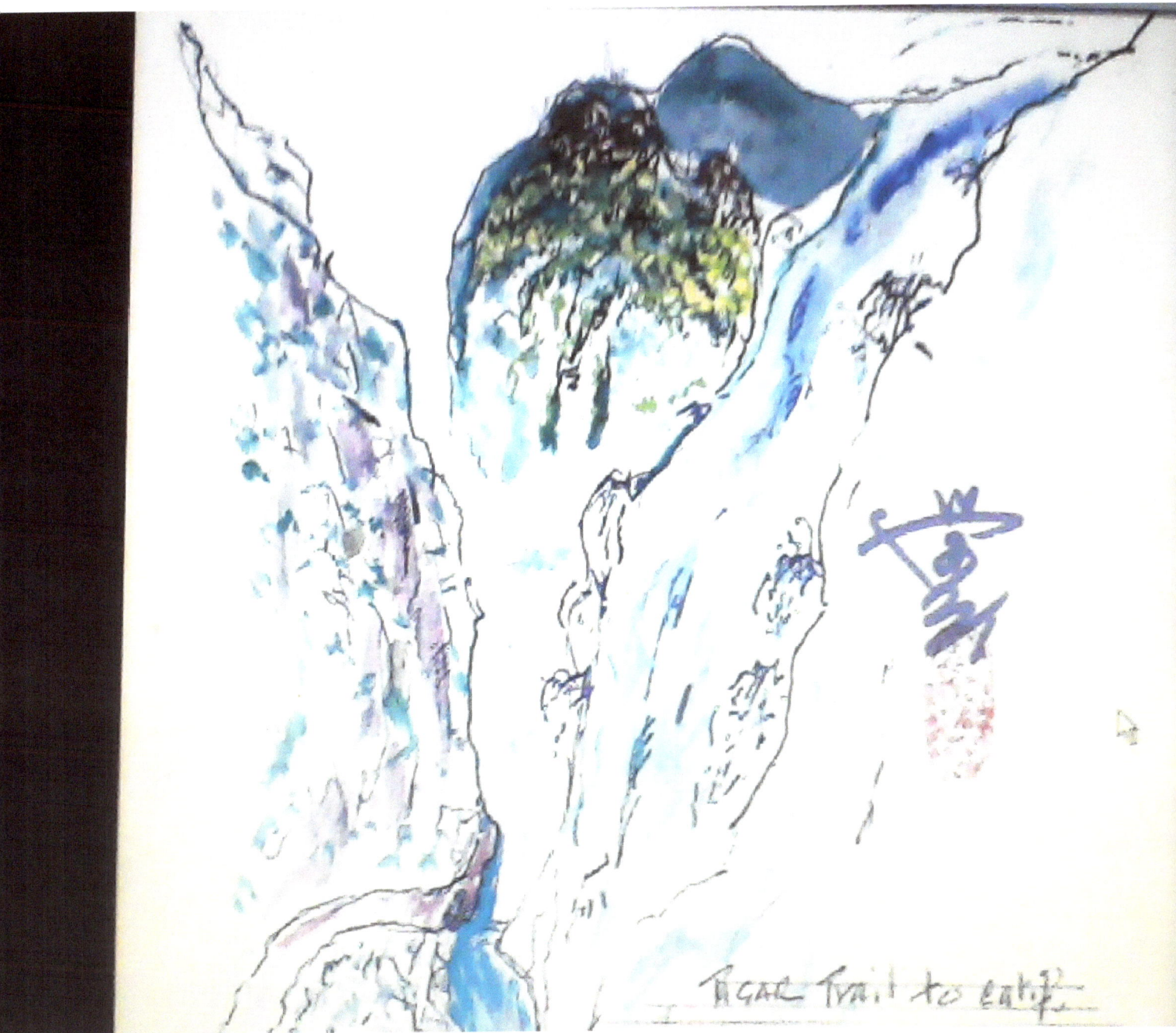

Tiger Trail to cabin

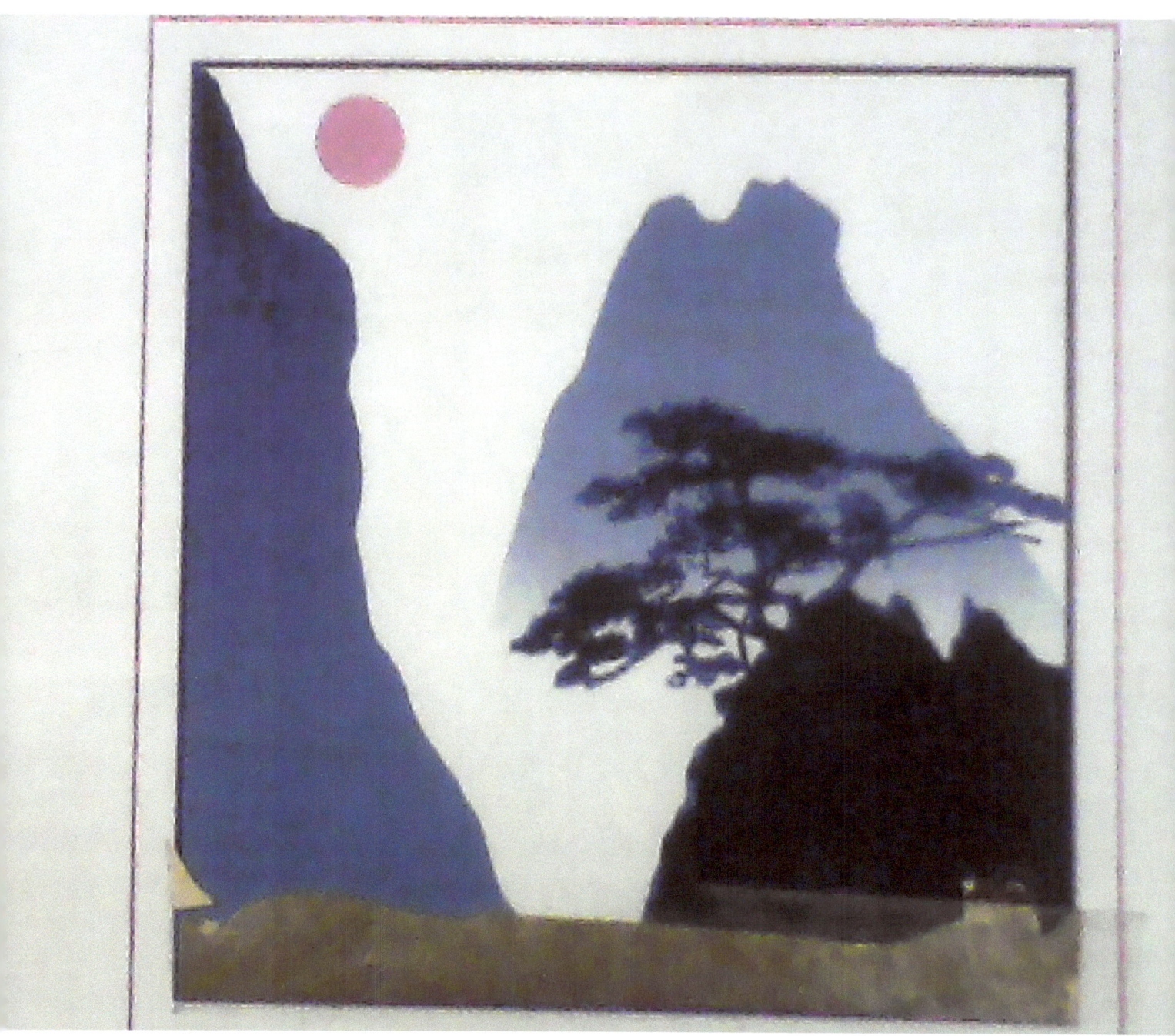

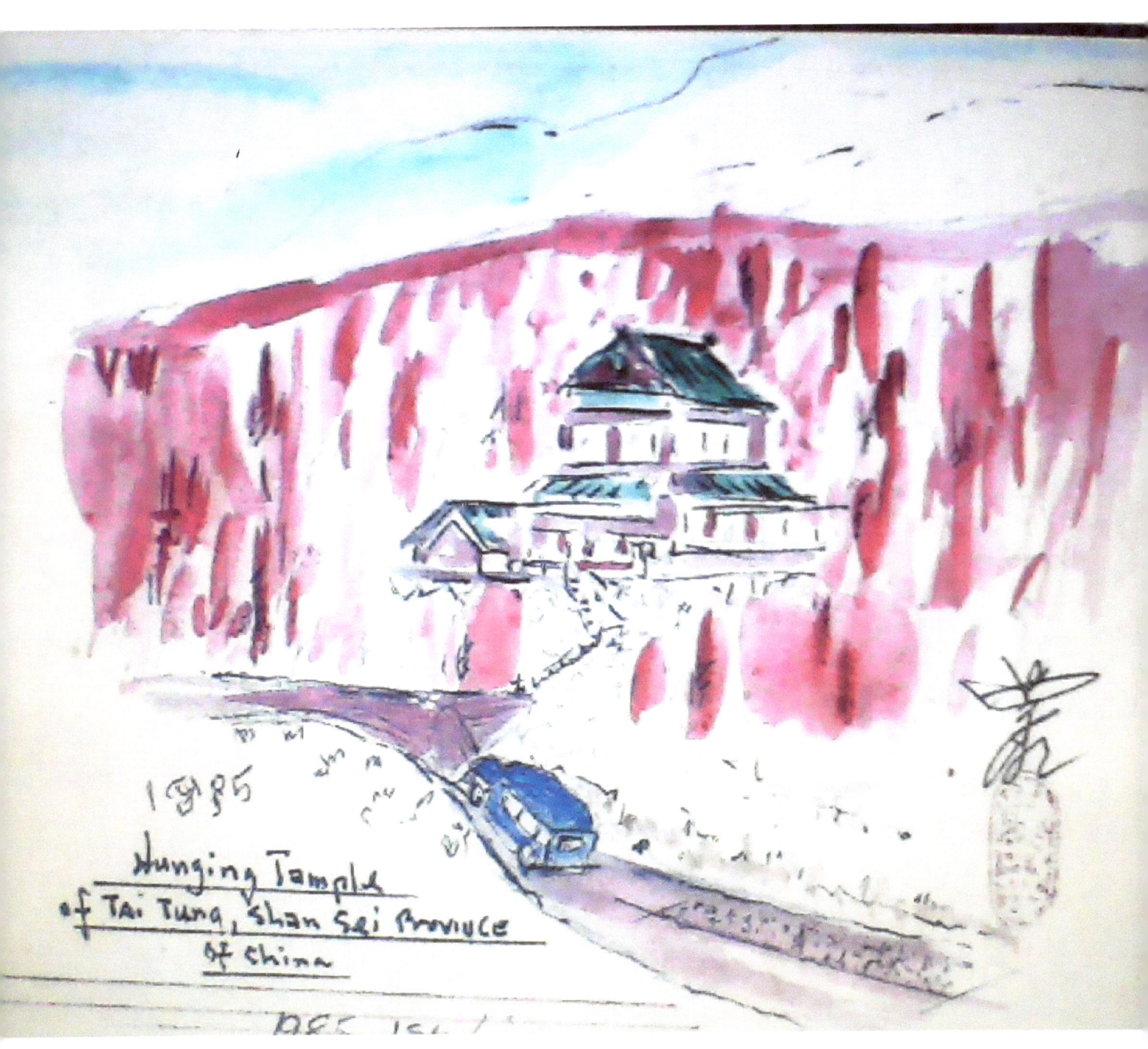

1985

Hanging Temple
of Tai Tung, Shan Sai Province
of China

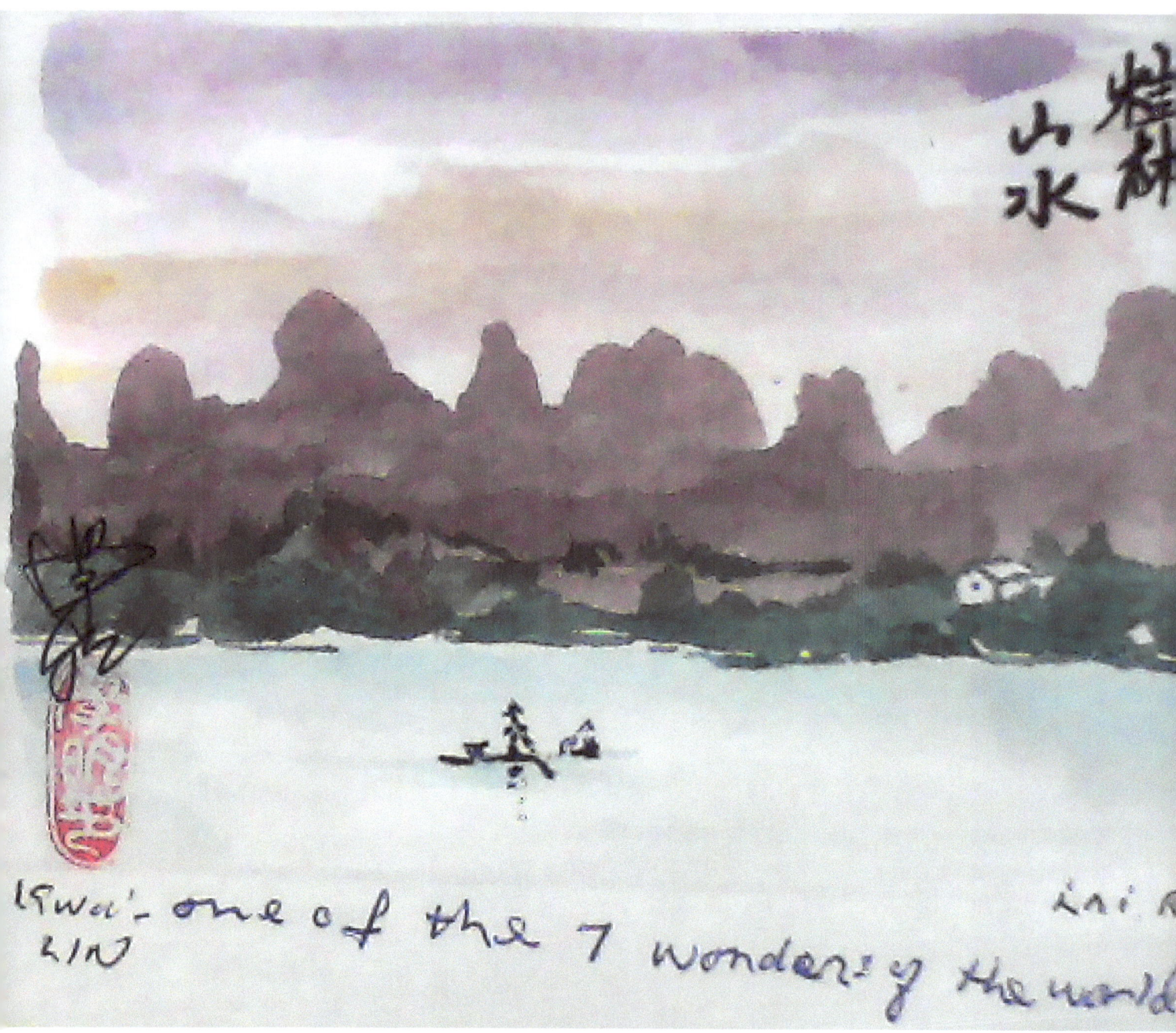

桂林
山水

Kwai - one of the 7 wonders of the world

Lin R

LIN

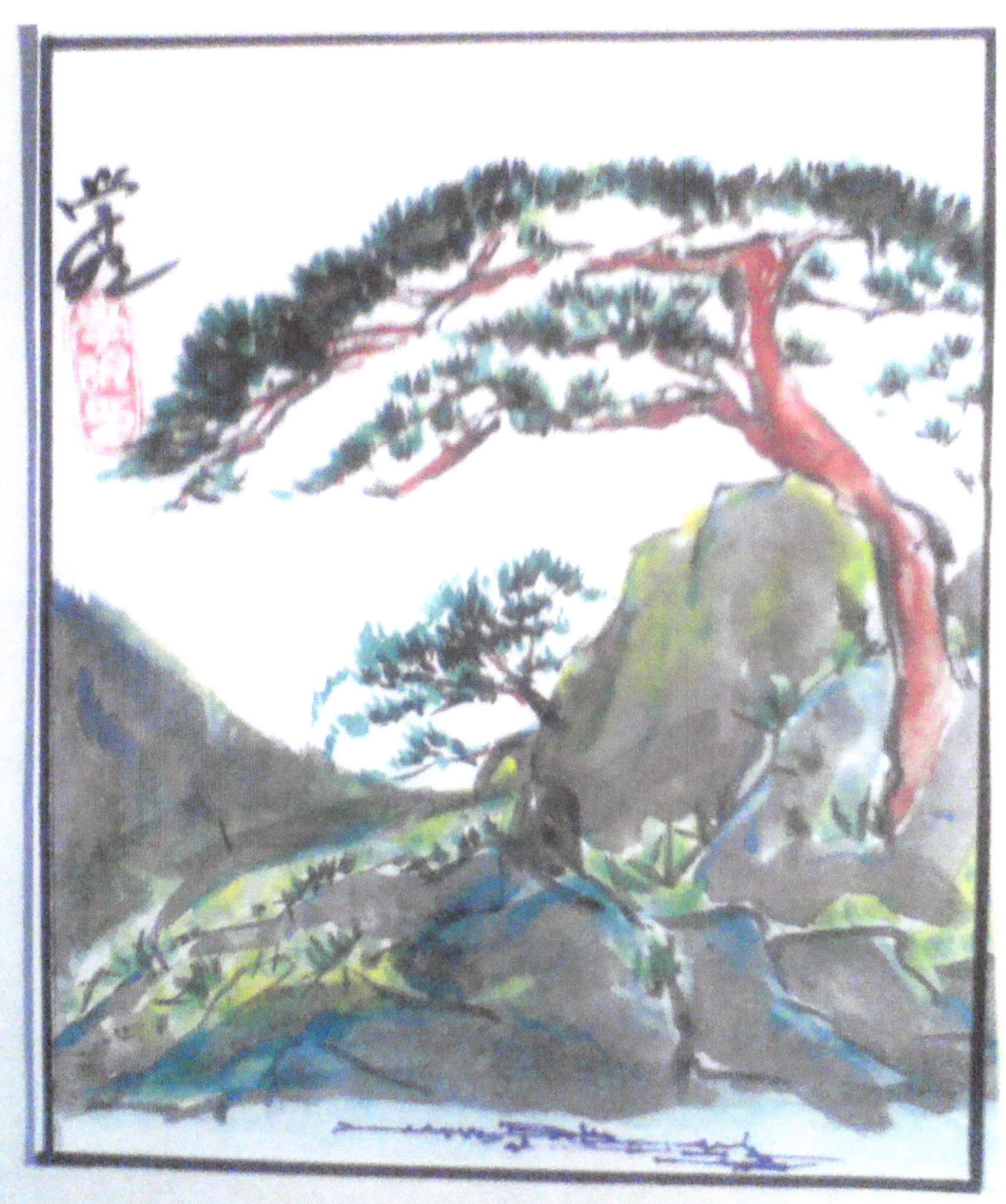

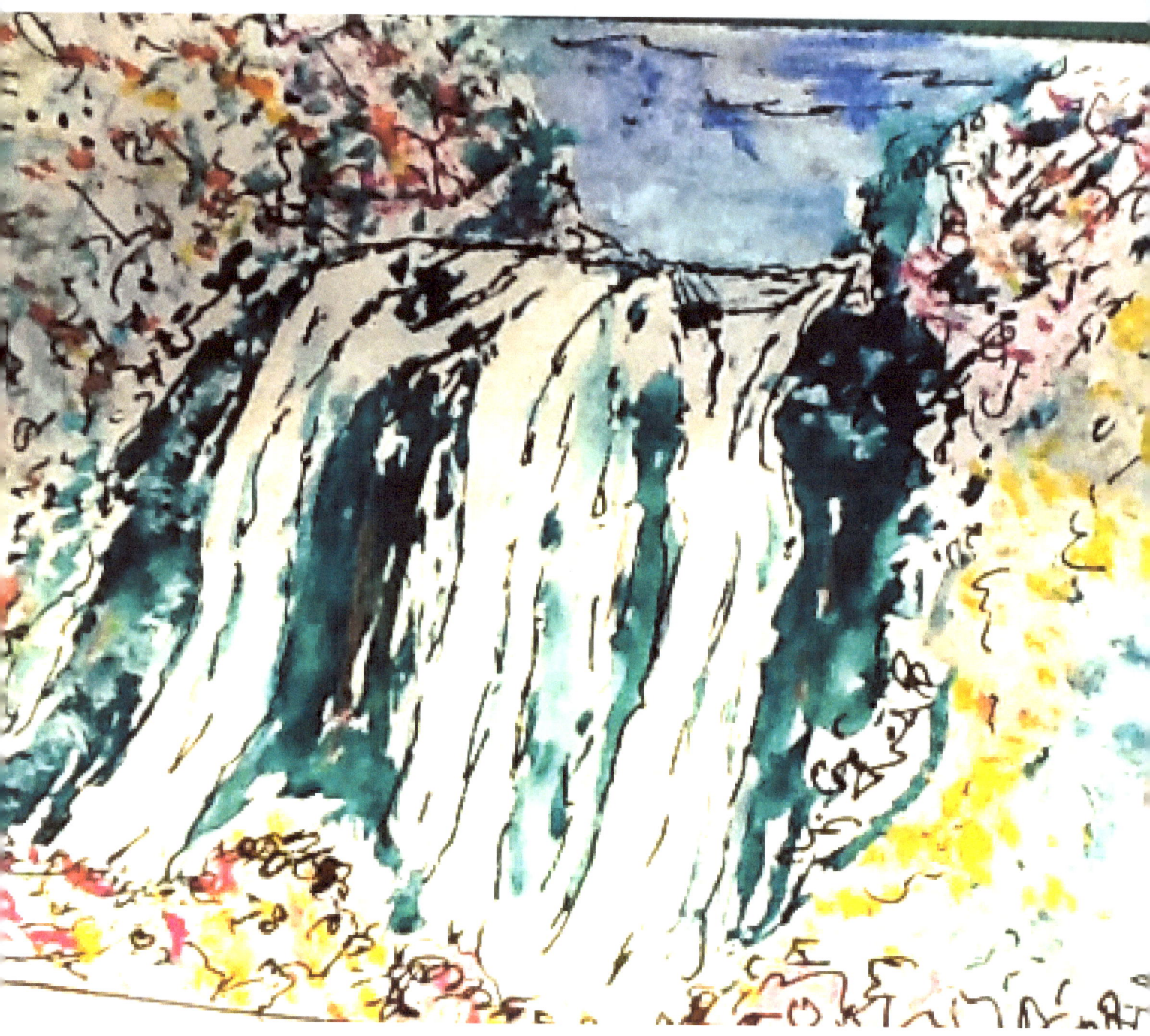

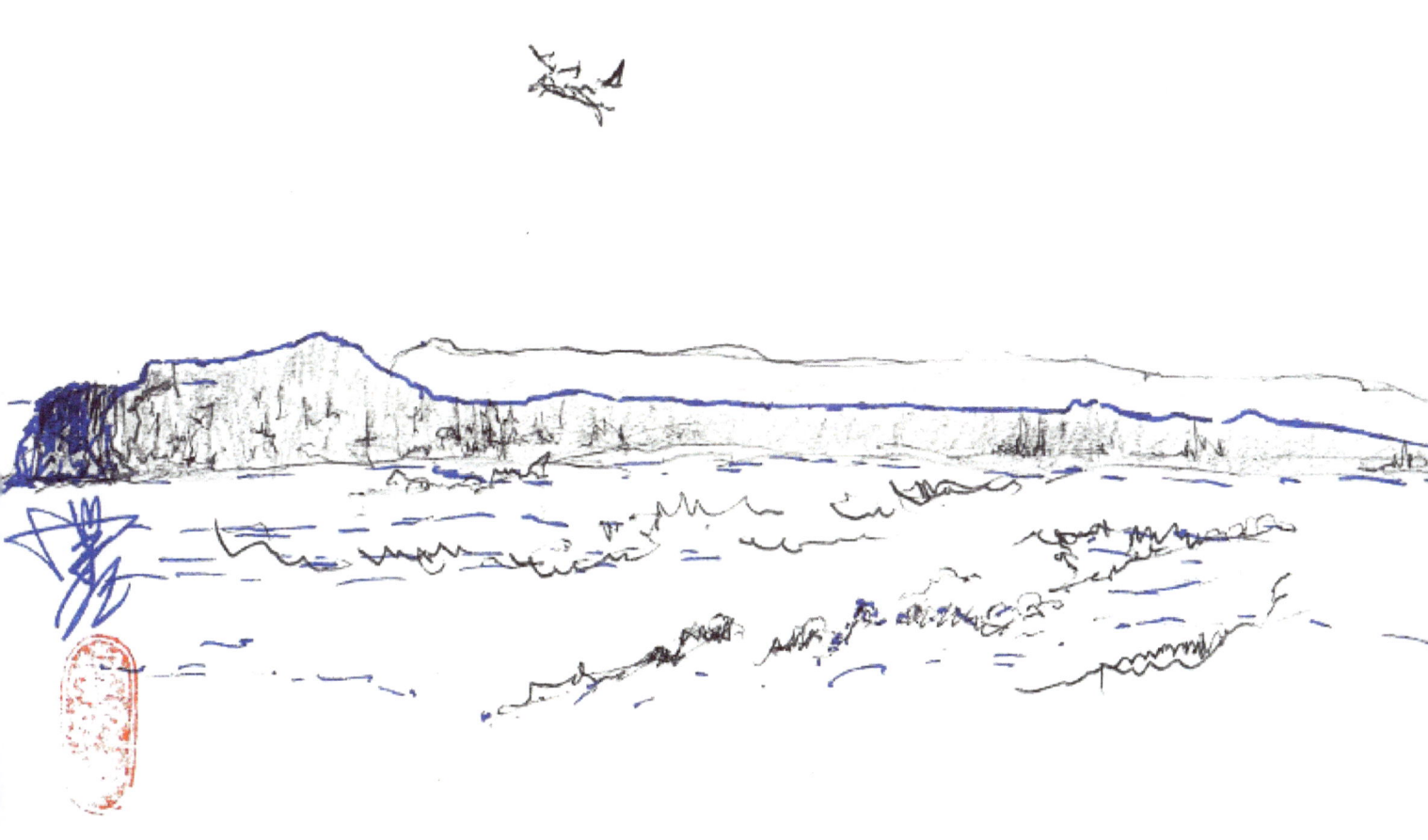

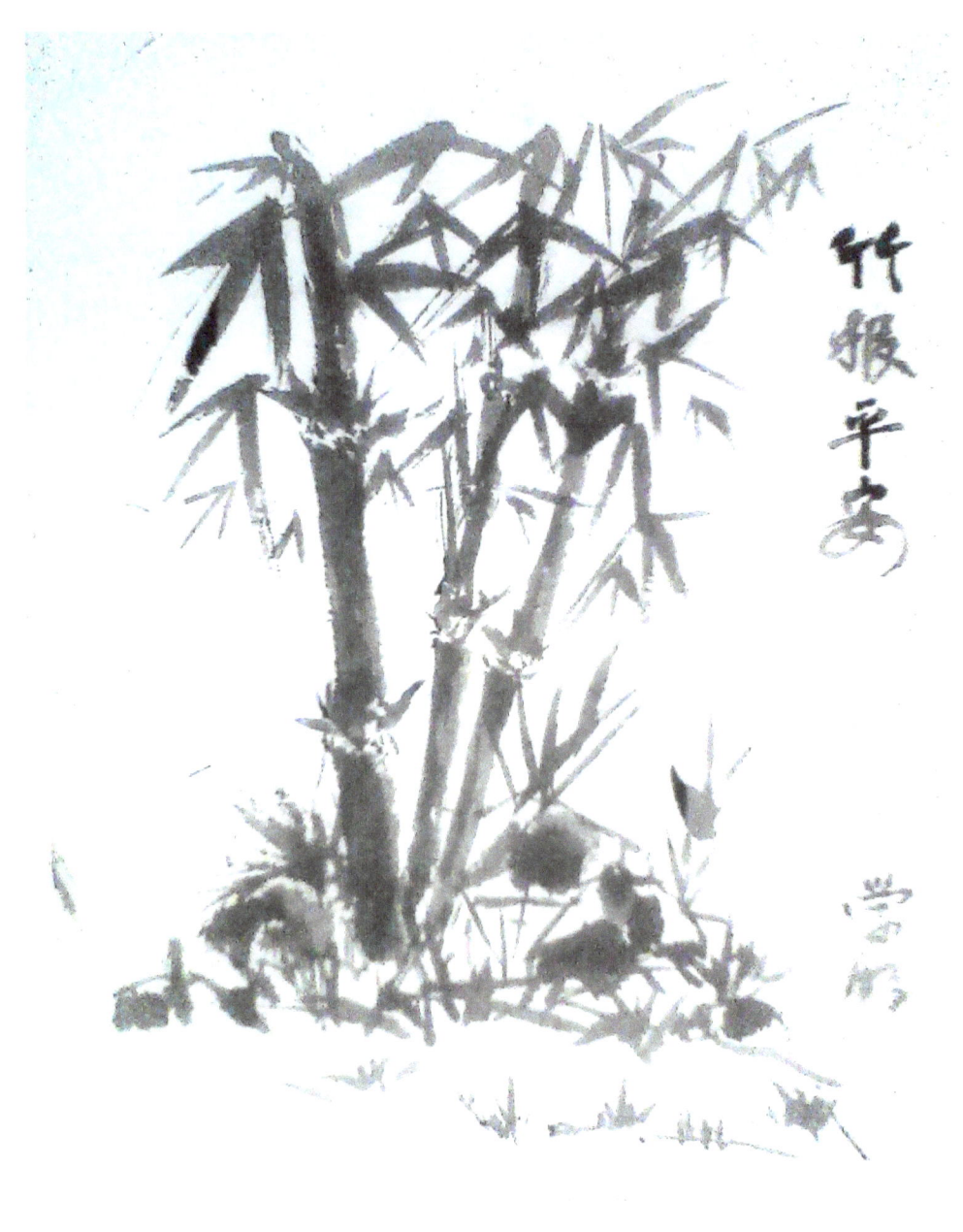

竹報平安

学群

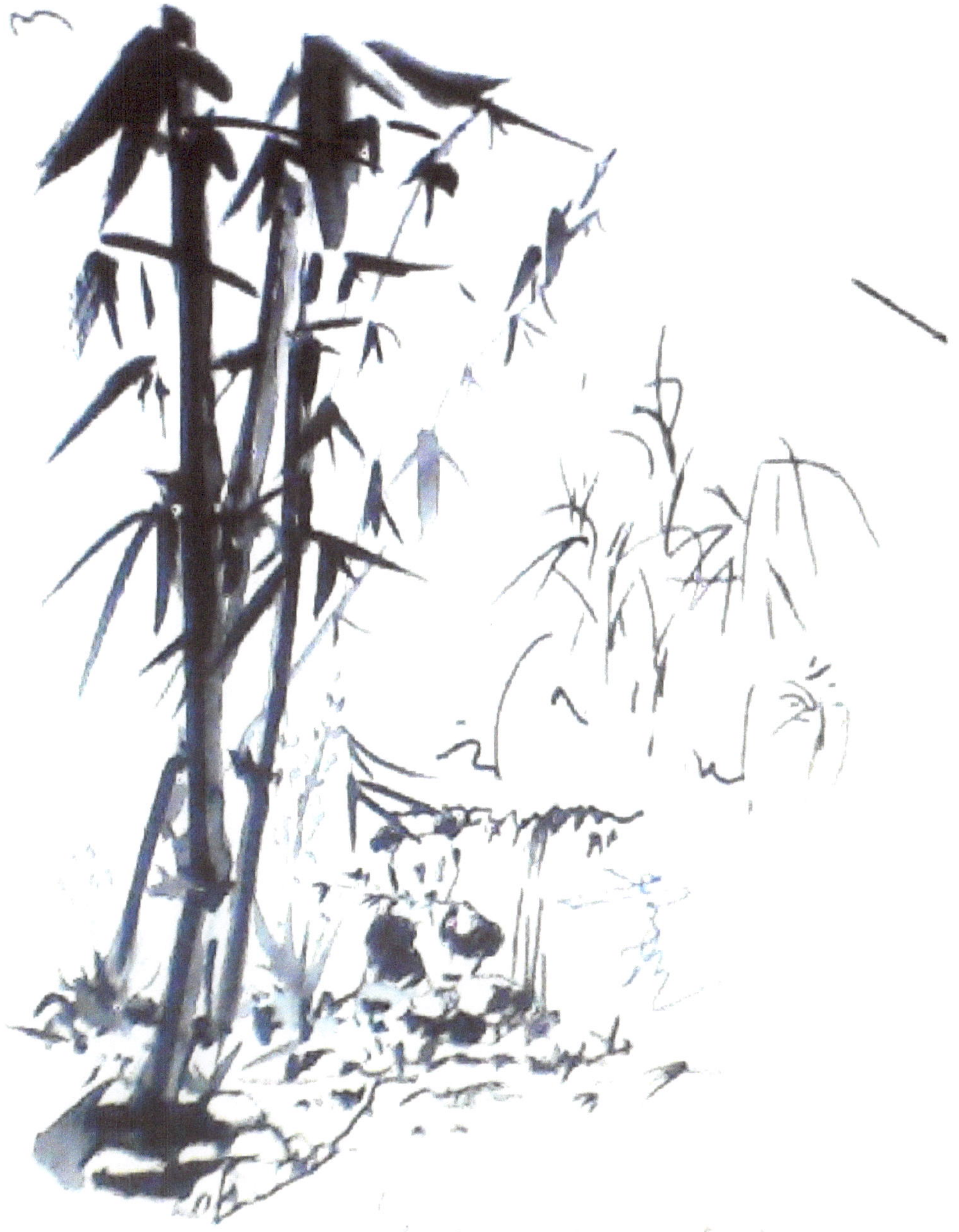

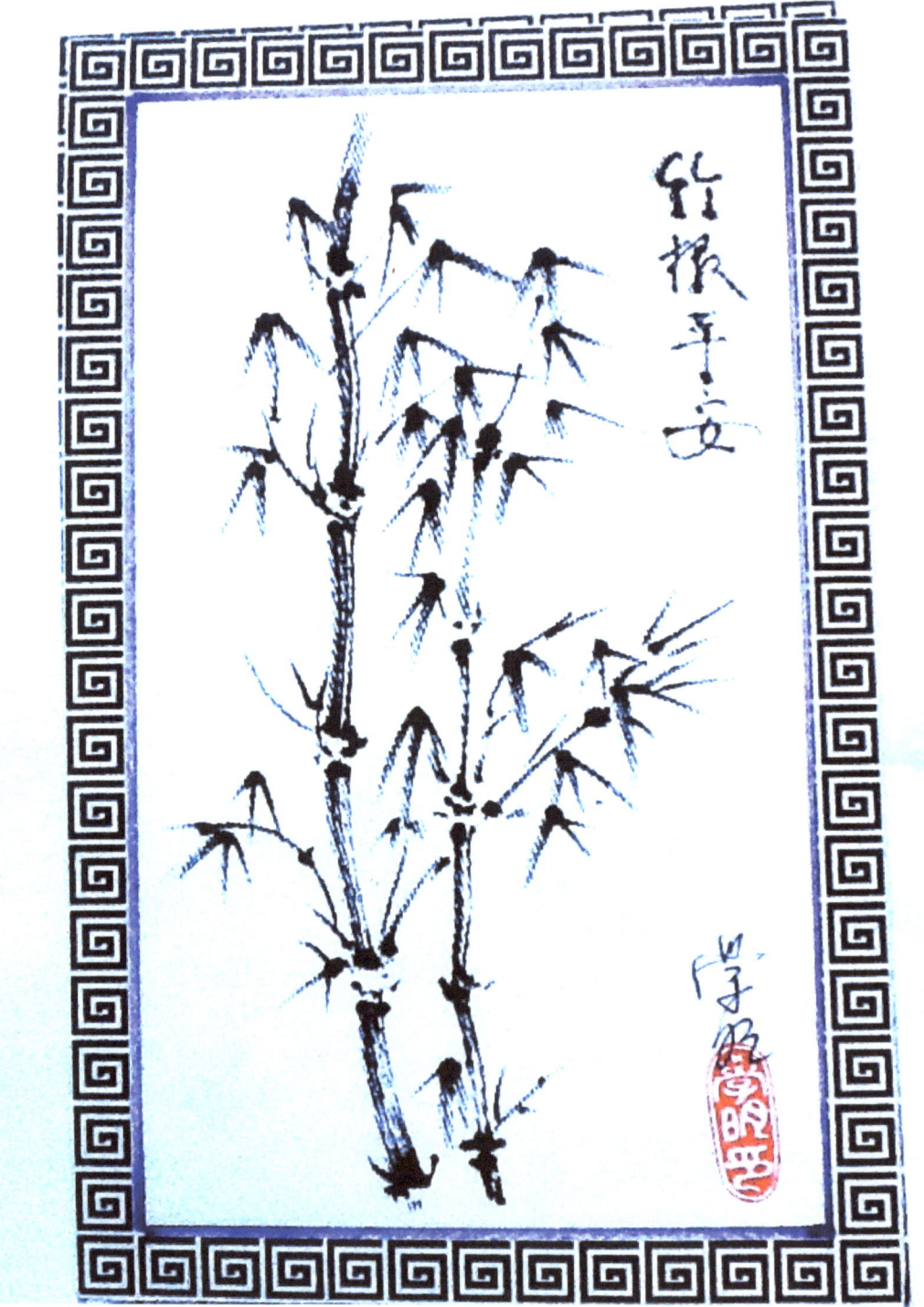

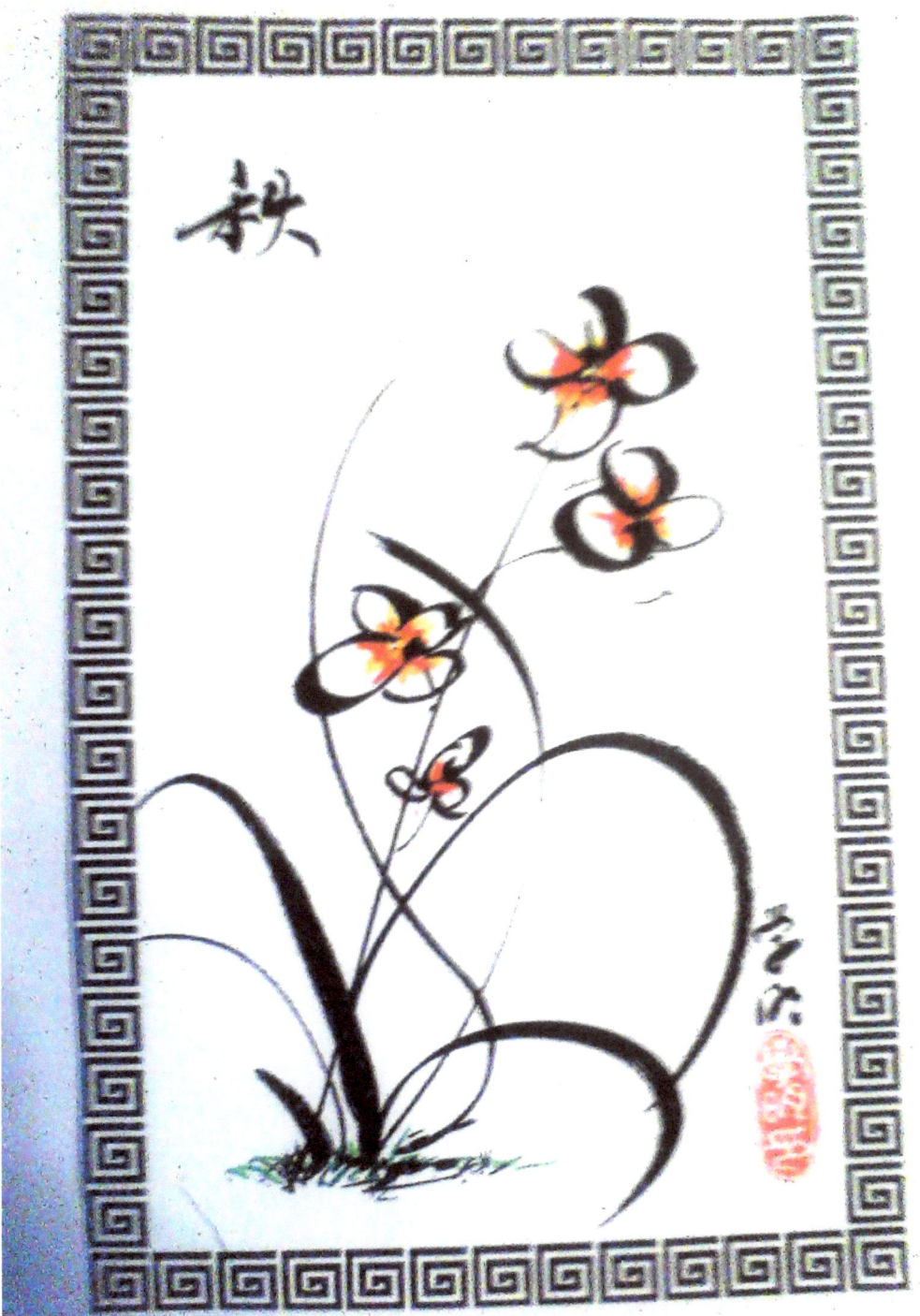

13

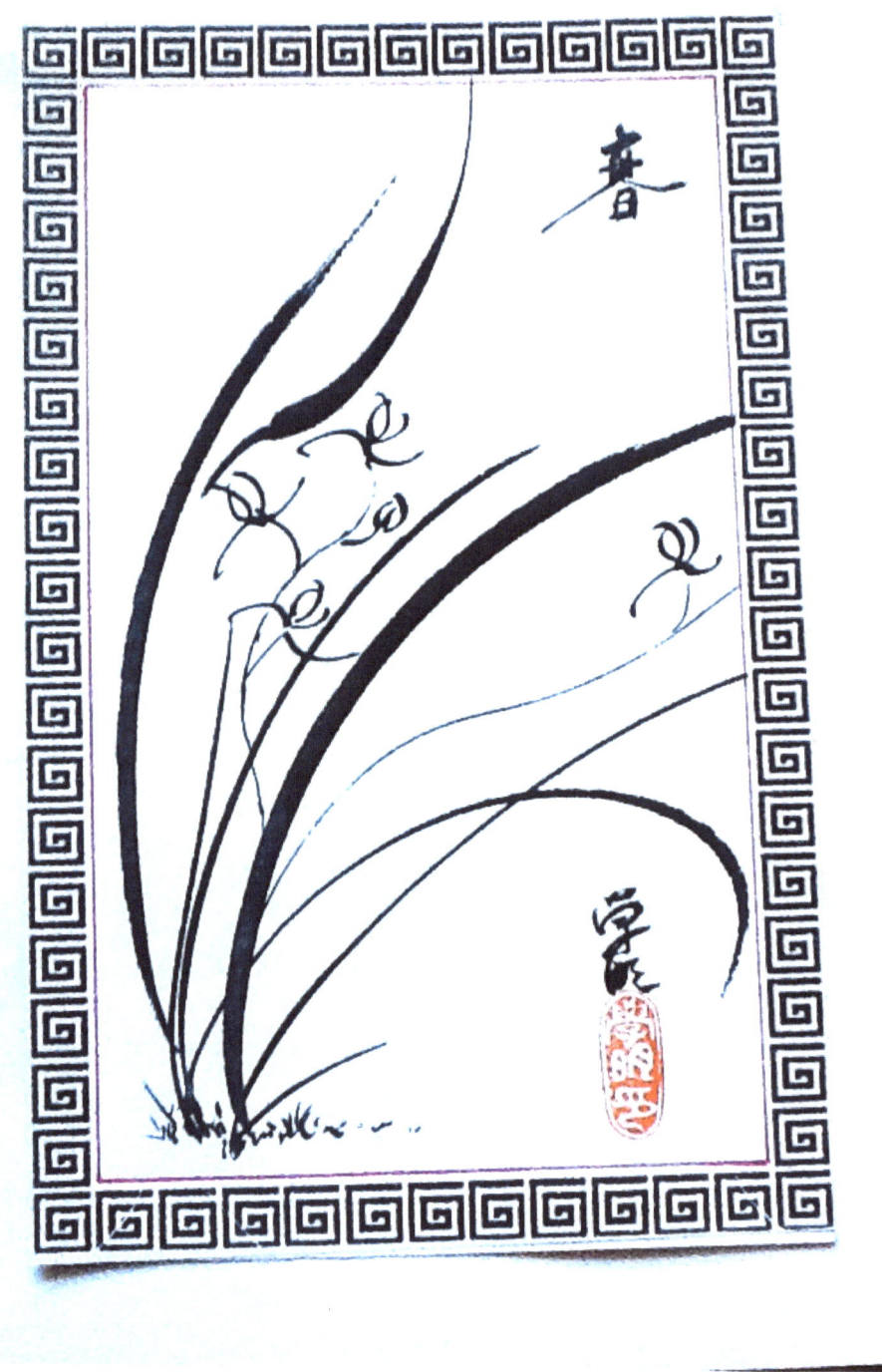

14

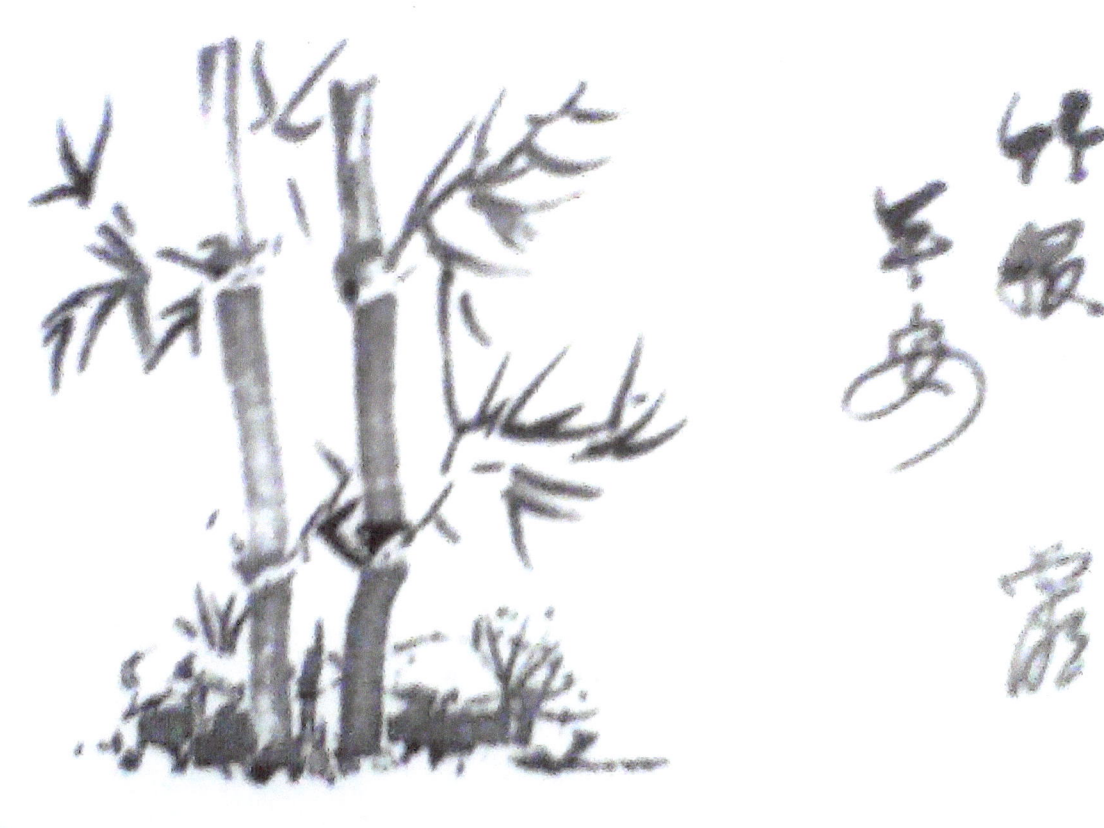

竹報
平安

蜀

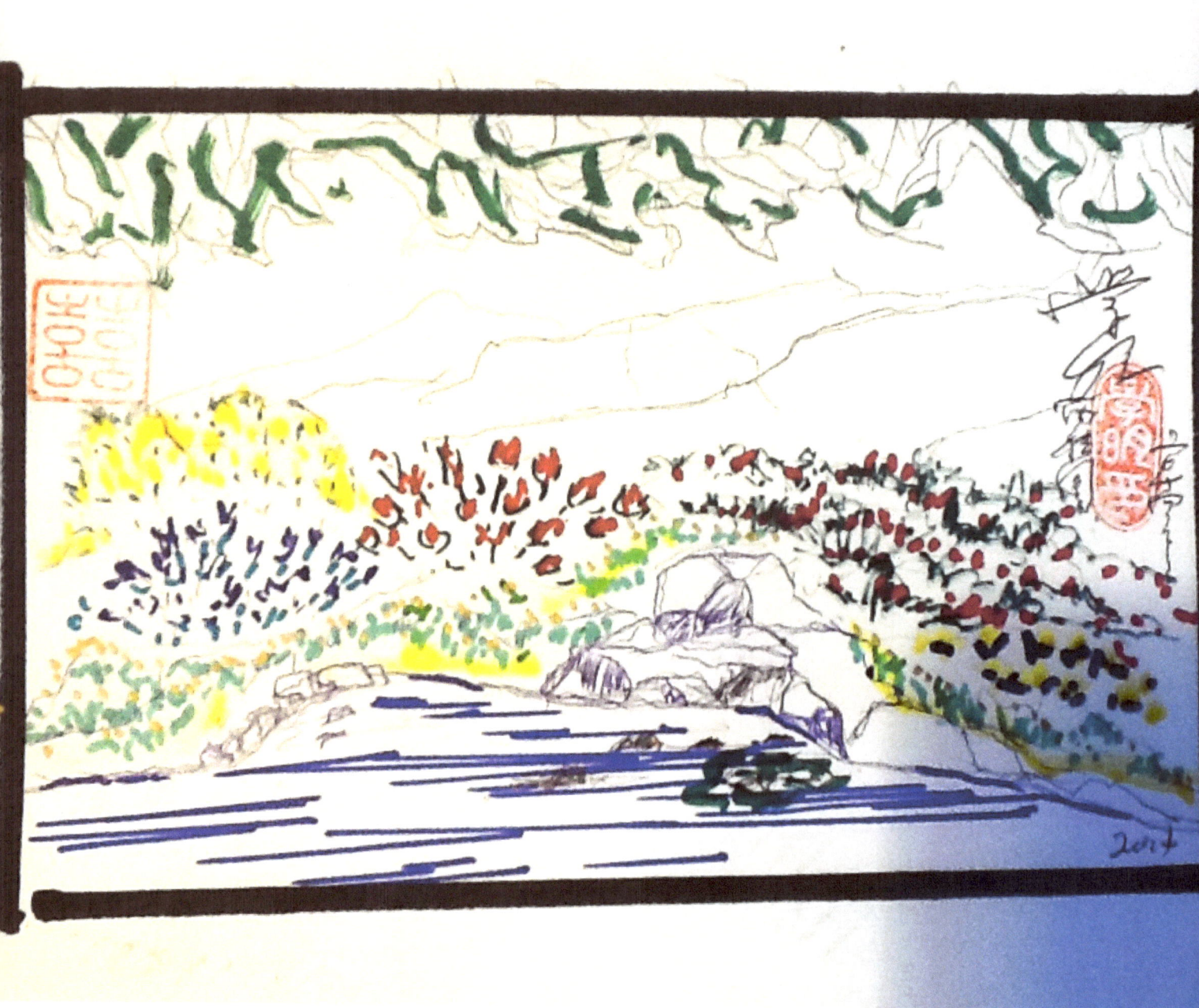

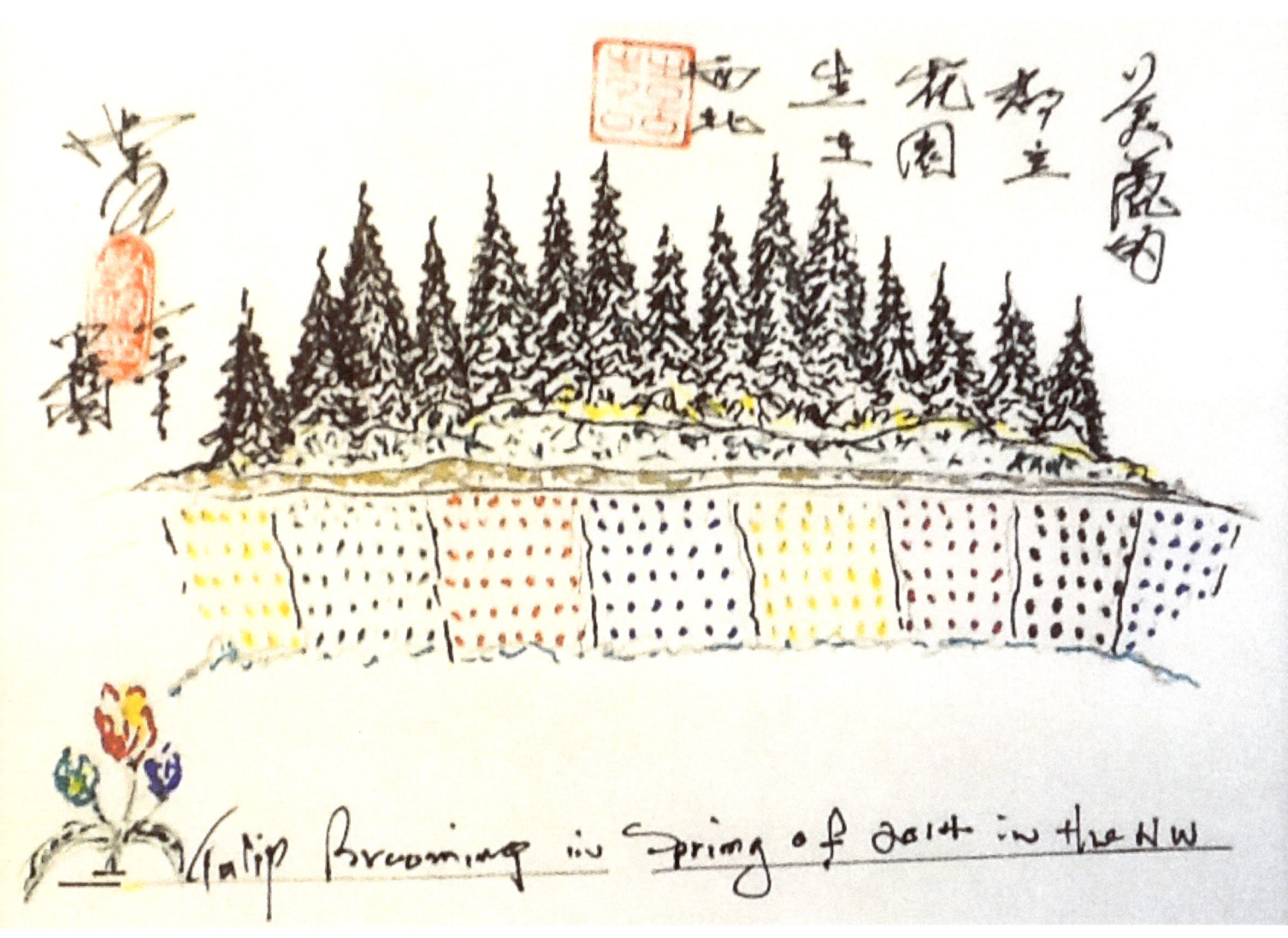

Tulip Brooming in Spring of 2014 in the NW

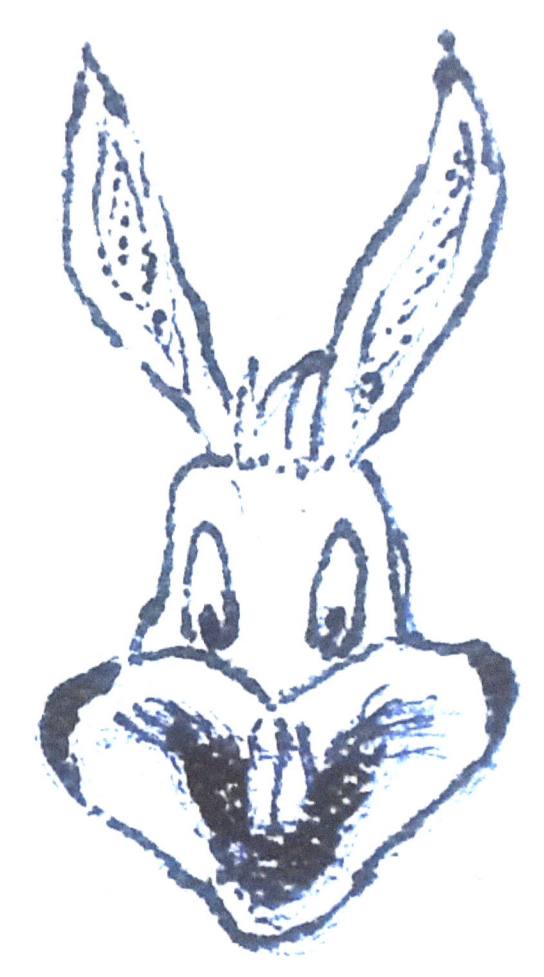

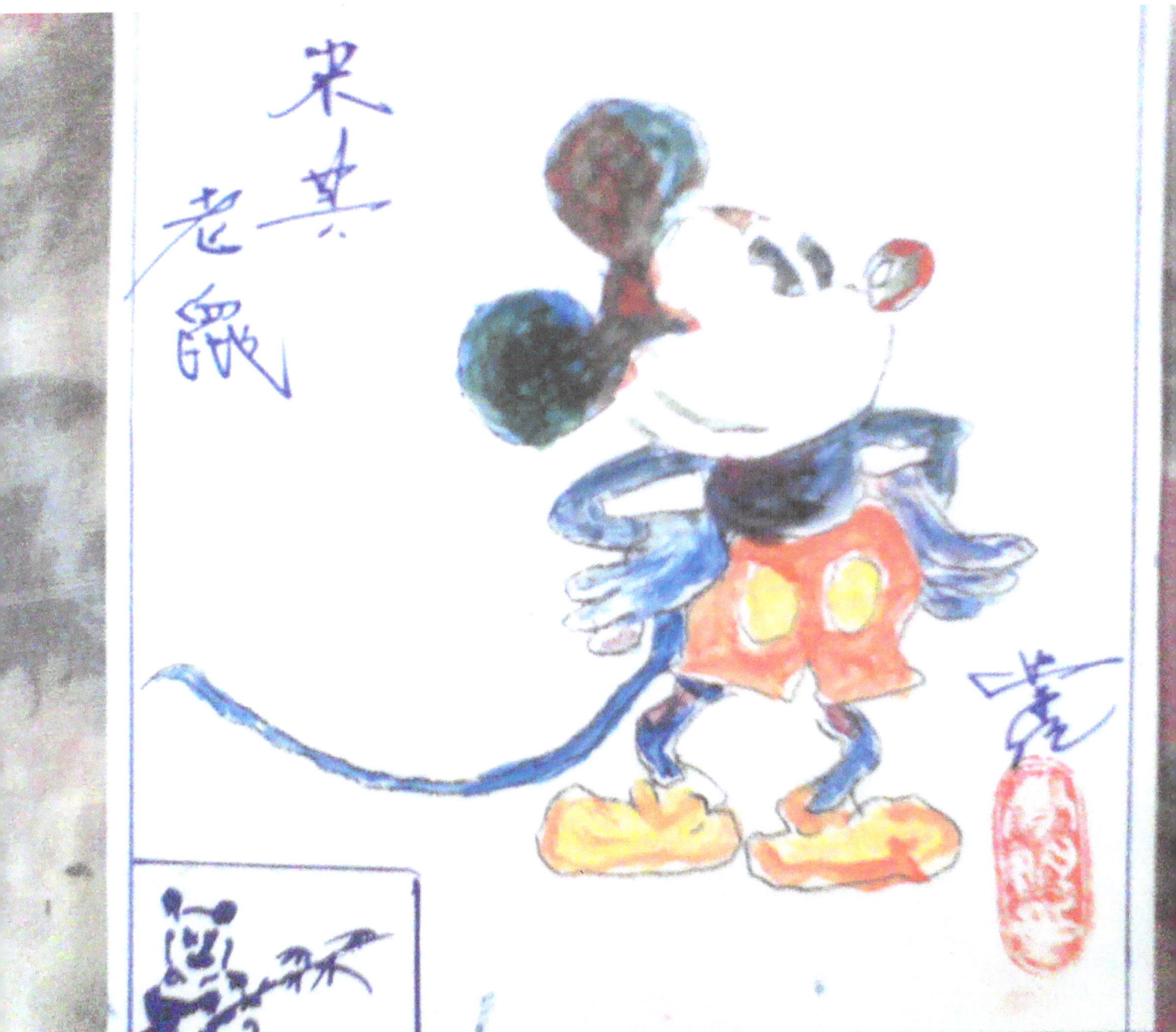

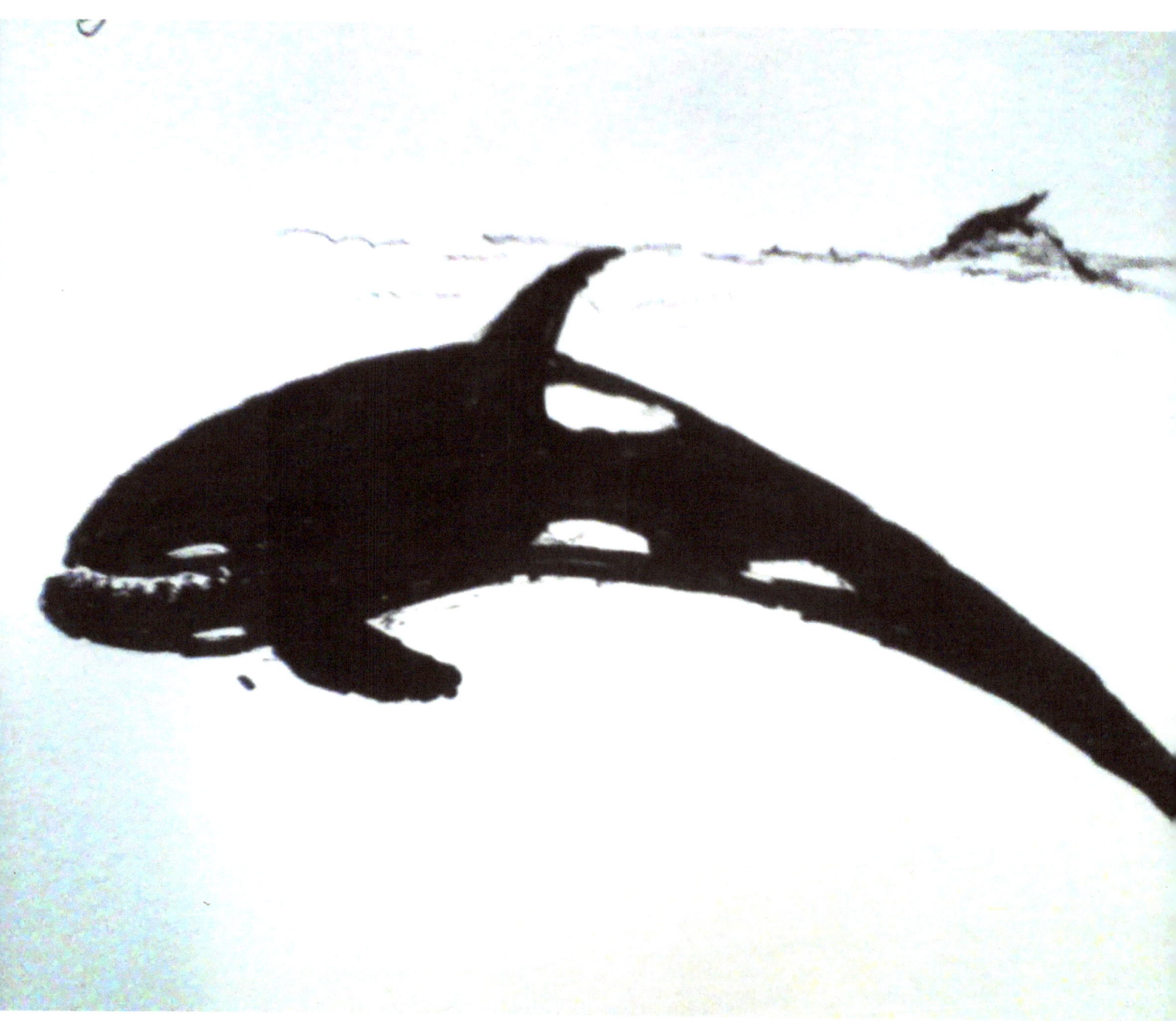

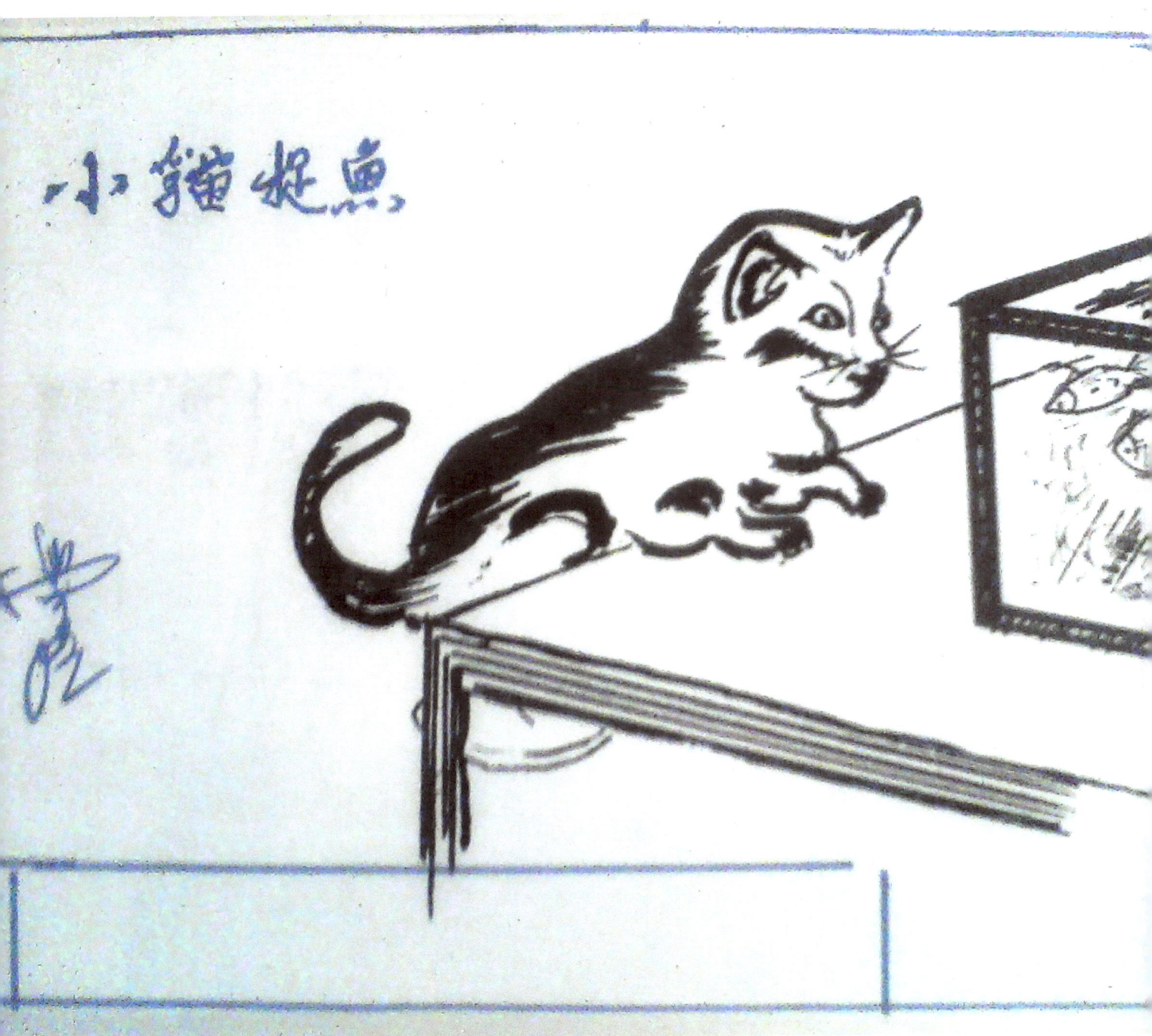

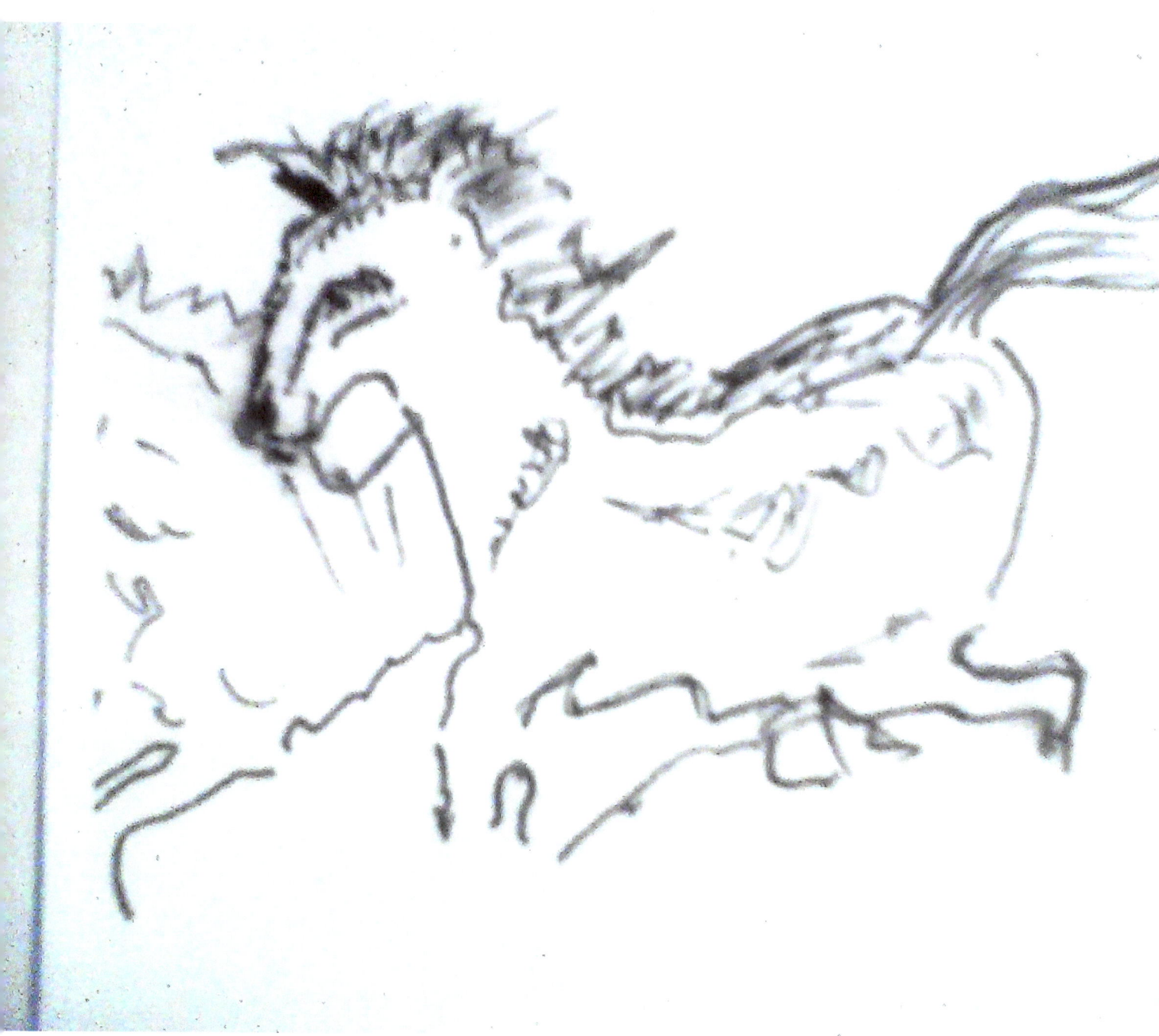

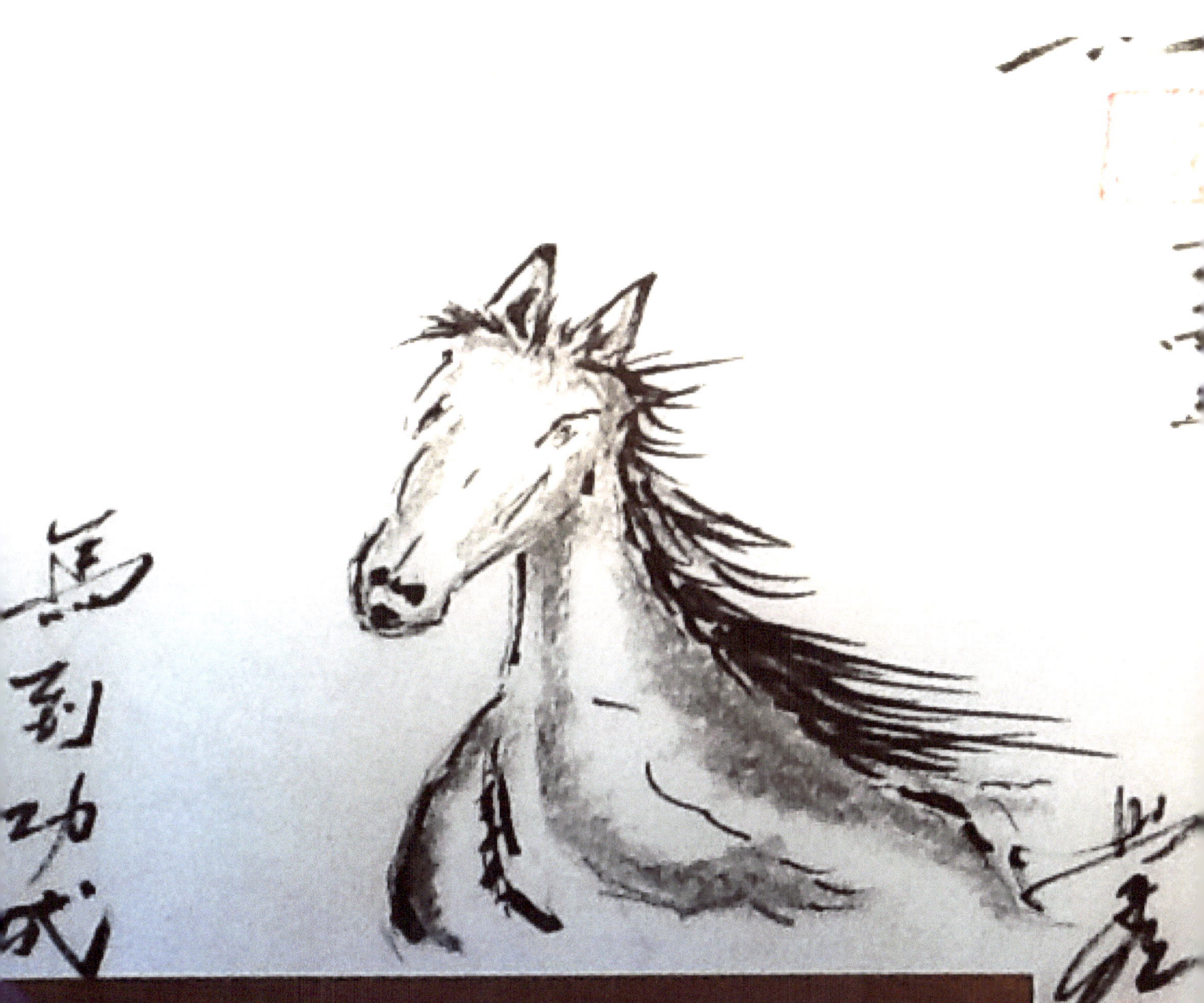

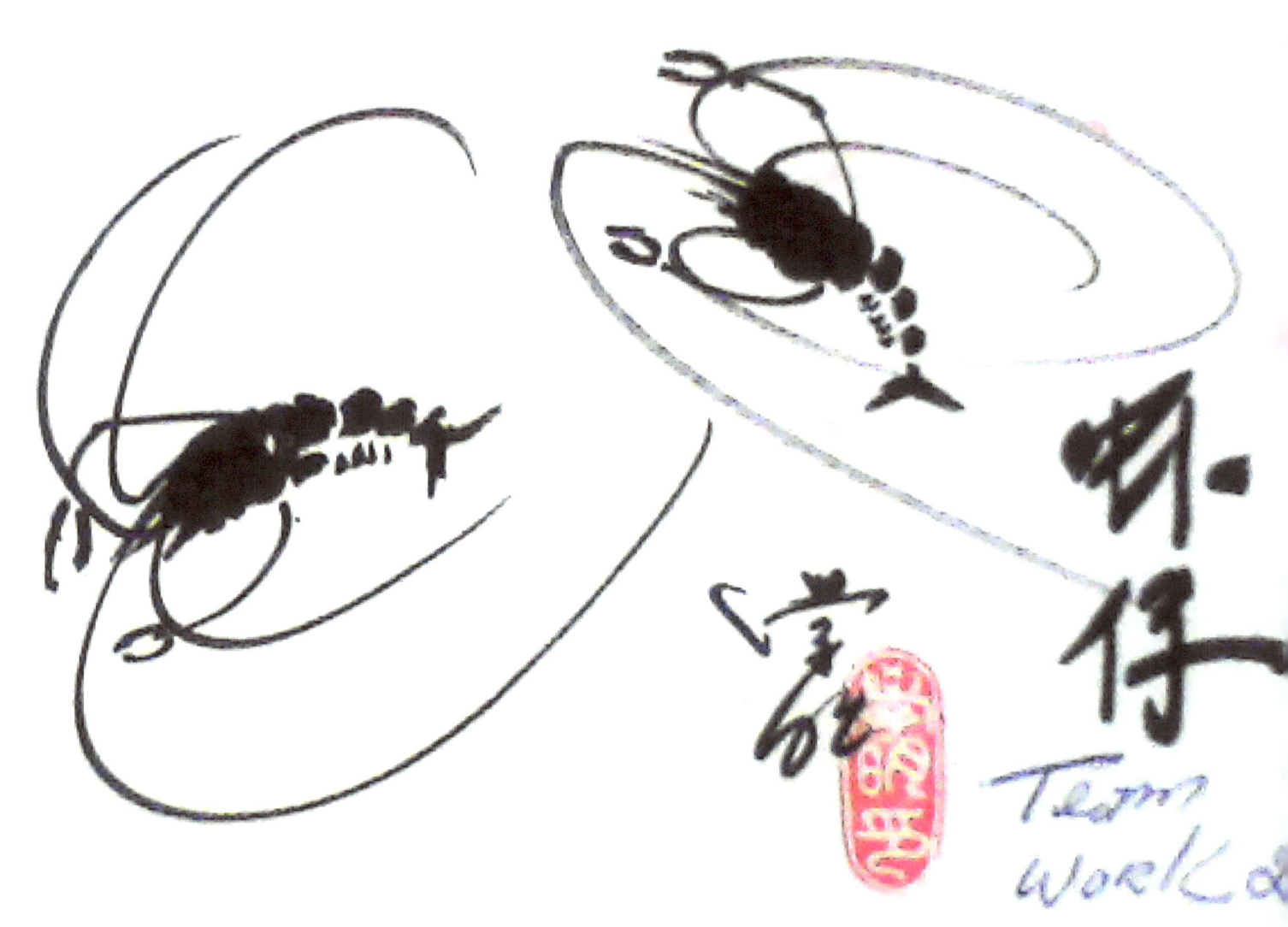

虾仔

寧

Team
World

龍光何富華

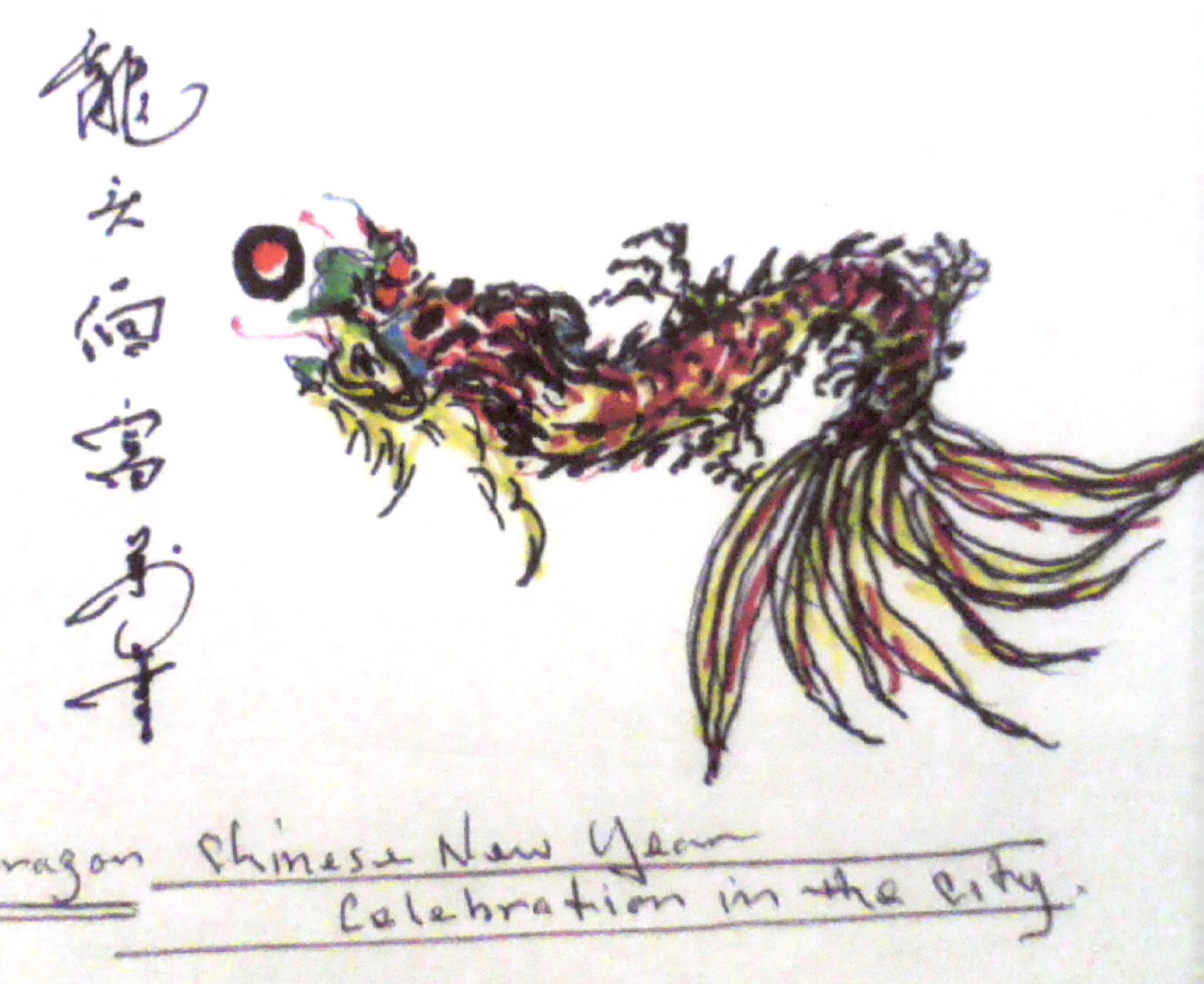

Dragon Chinese New Year
Celebration in the city.

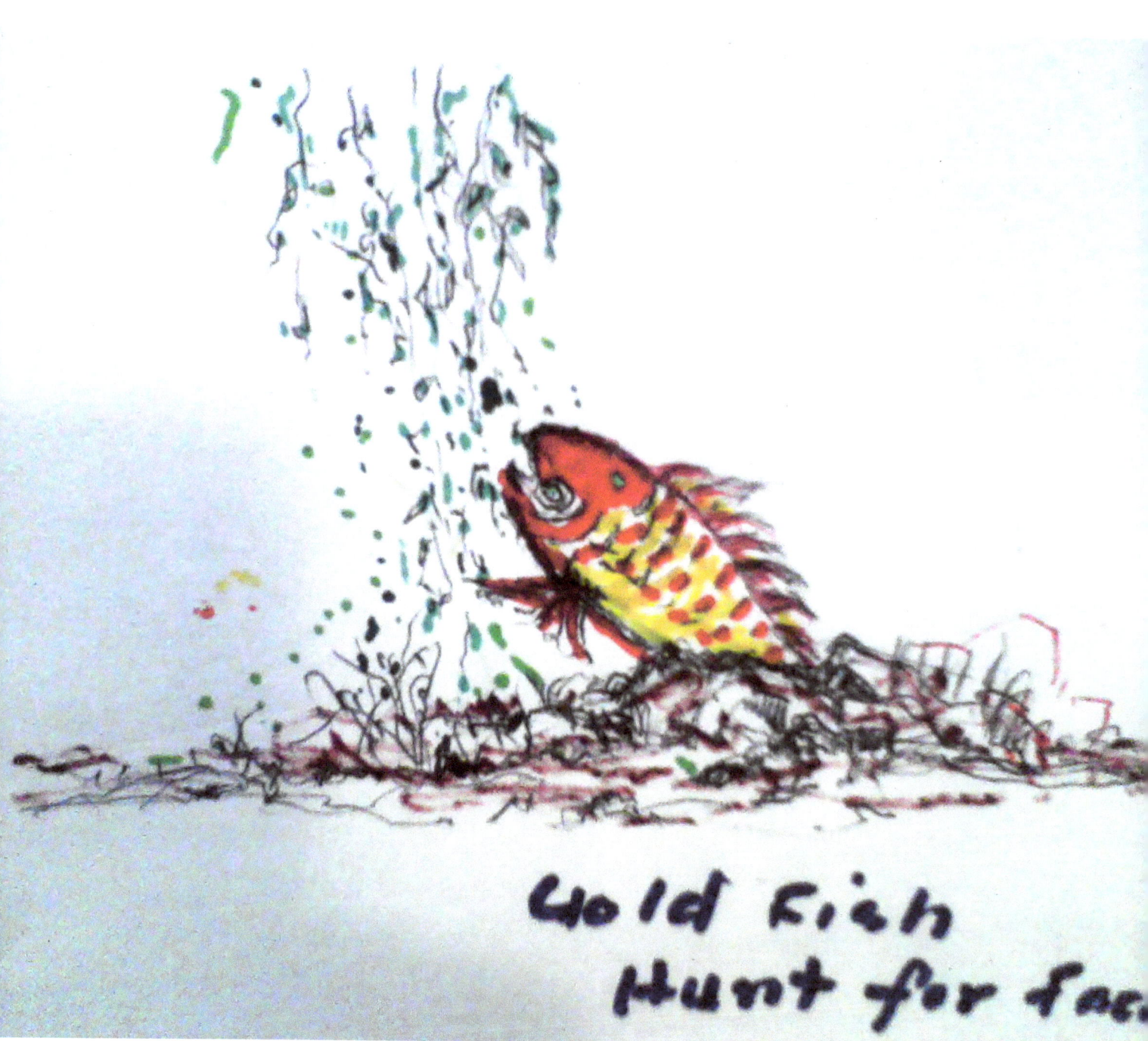

Uold Fish
Hunt for foo

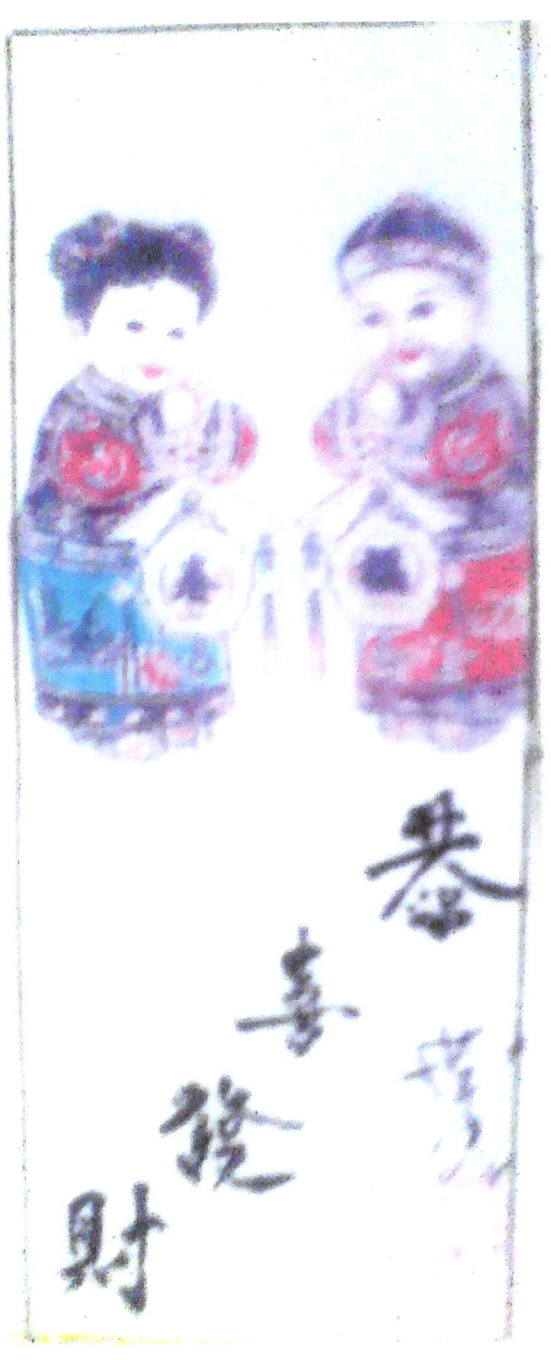

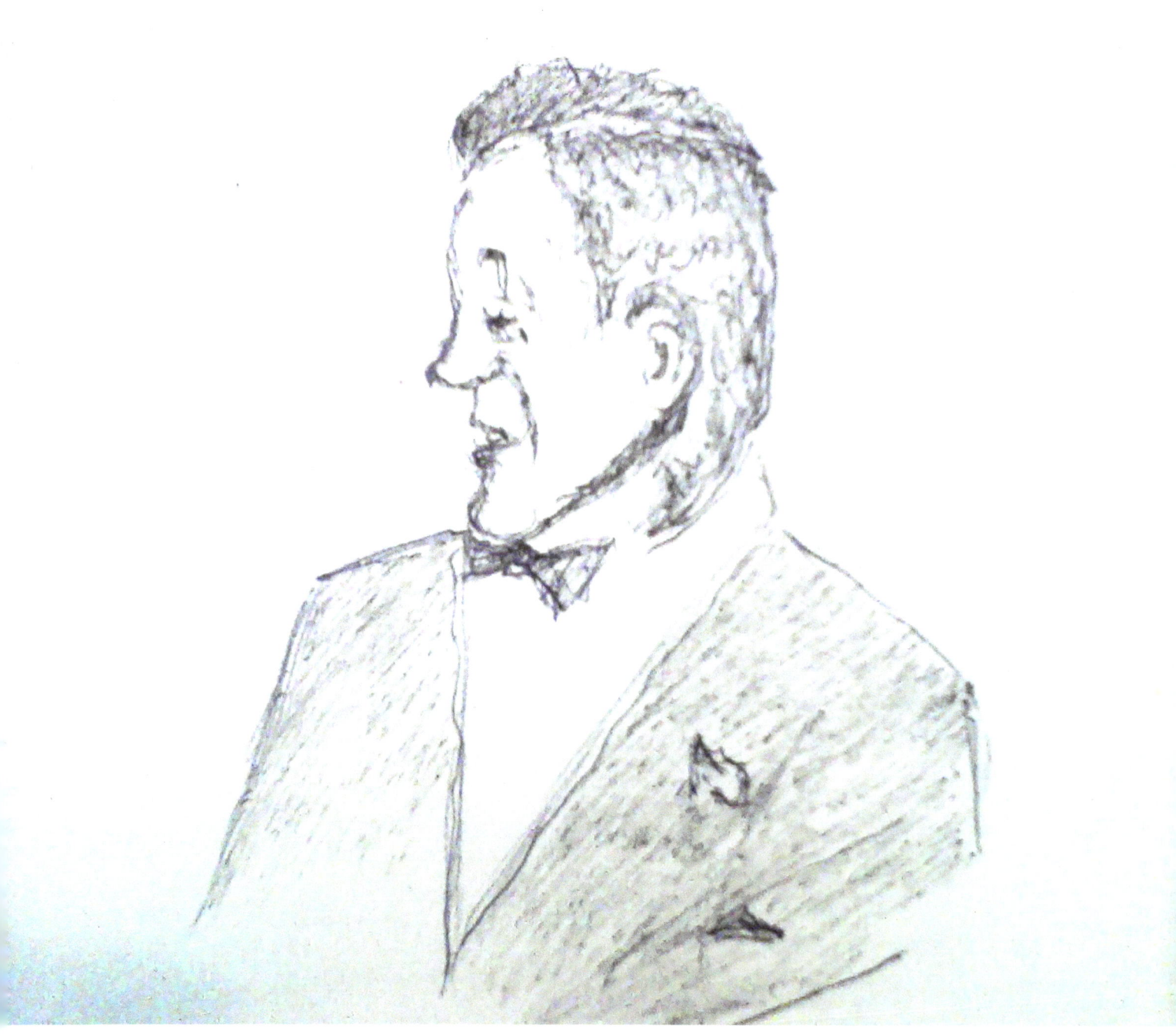

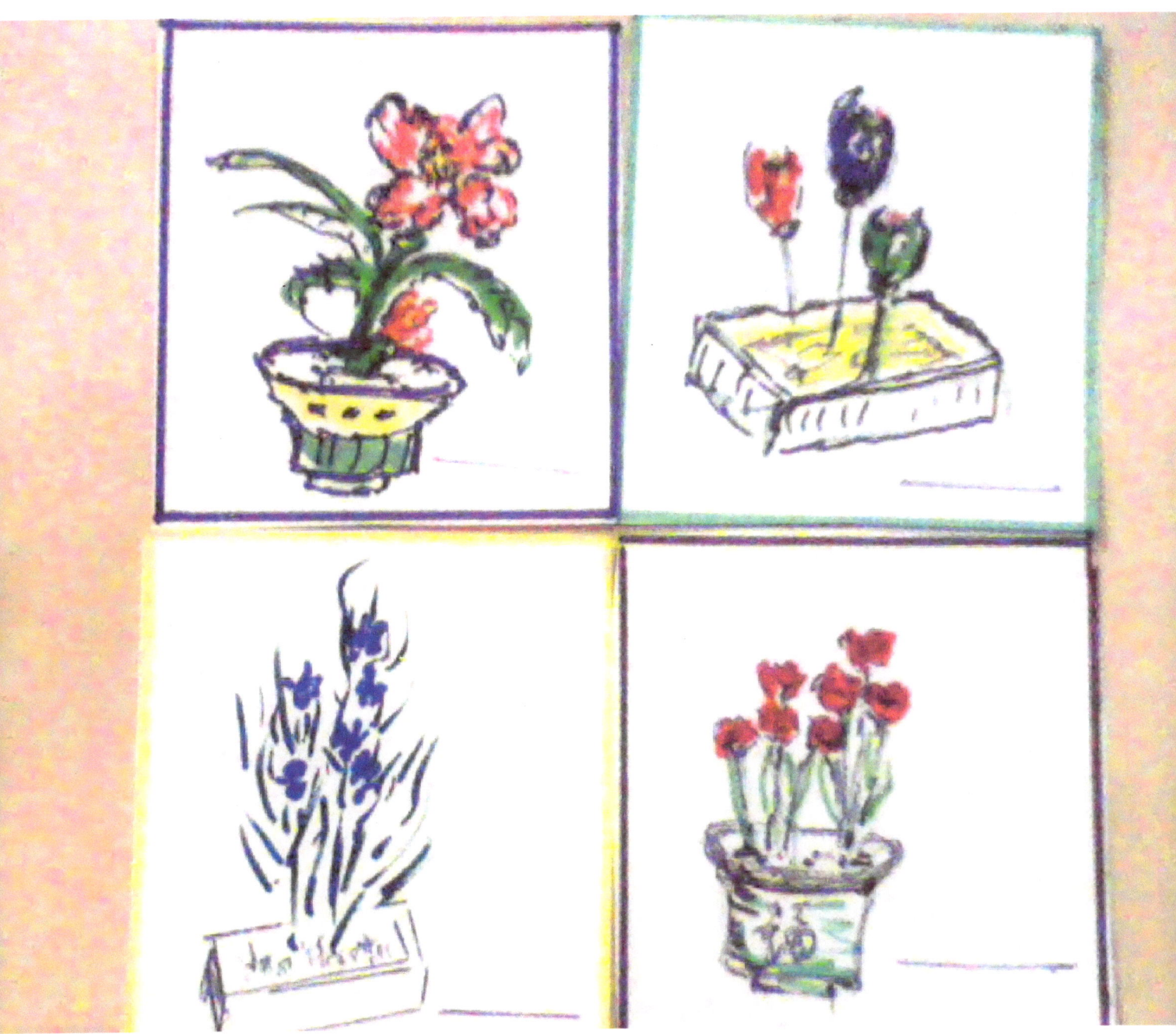

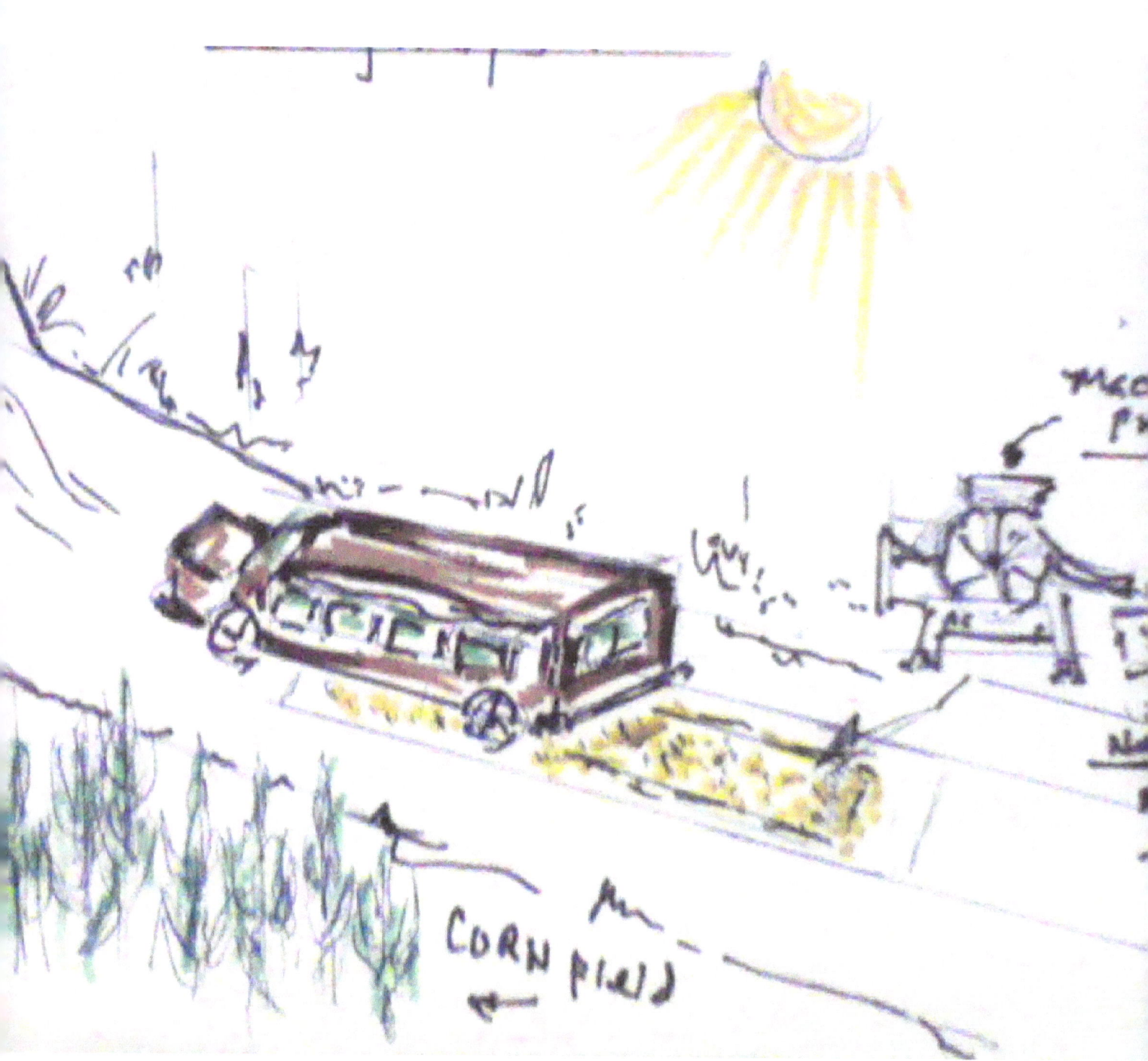

CORN field

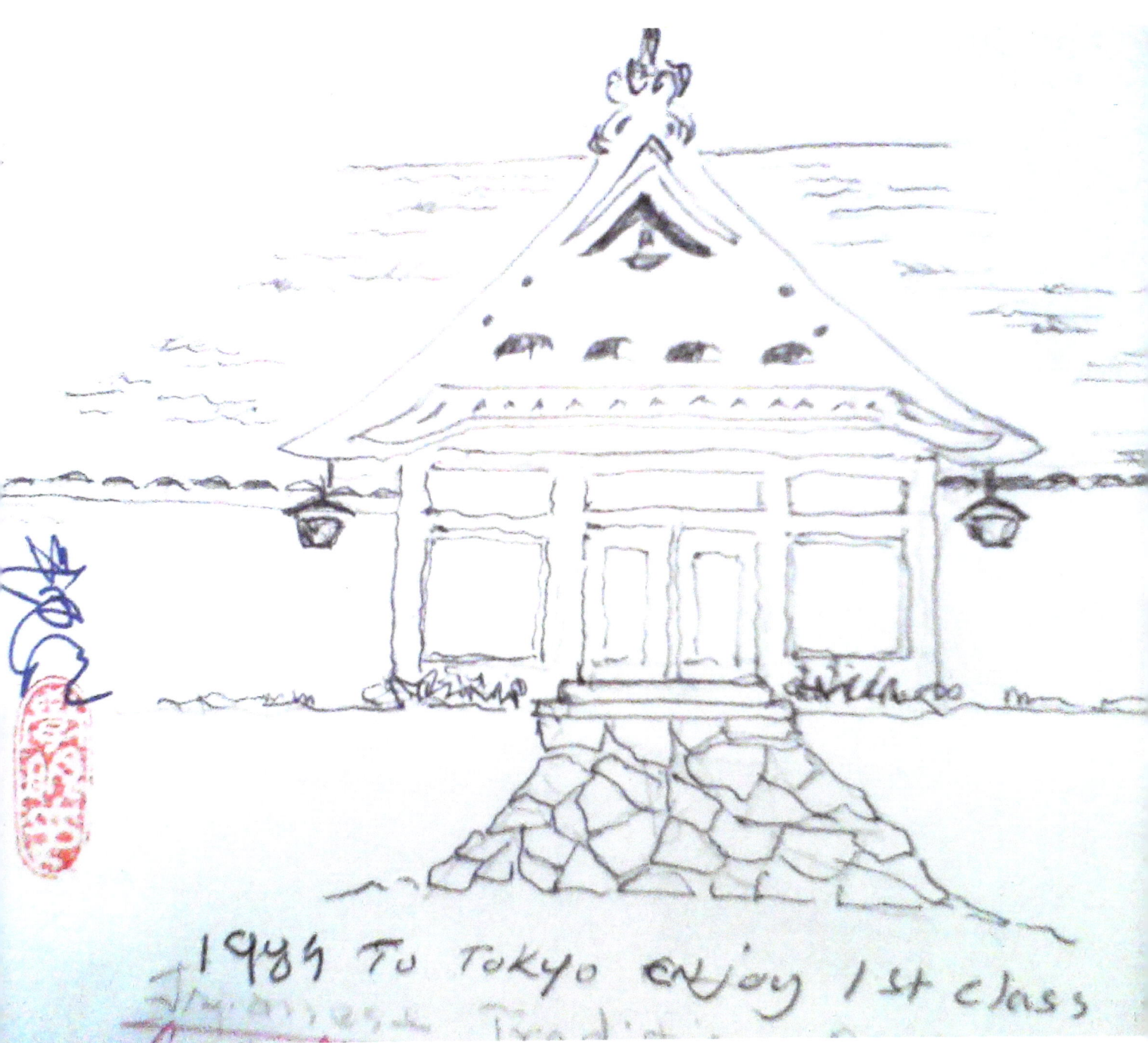

1989 To Tokyo enjoy 1st class
Japanese Tradition...

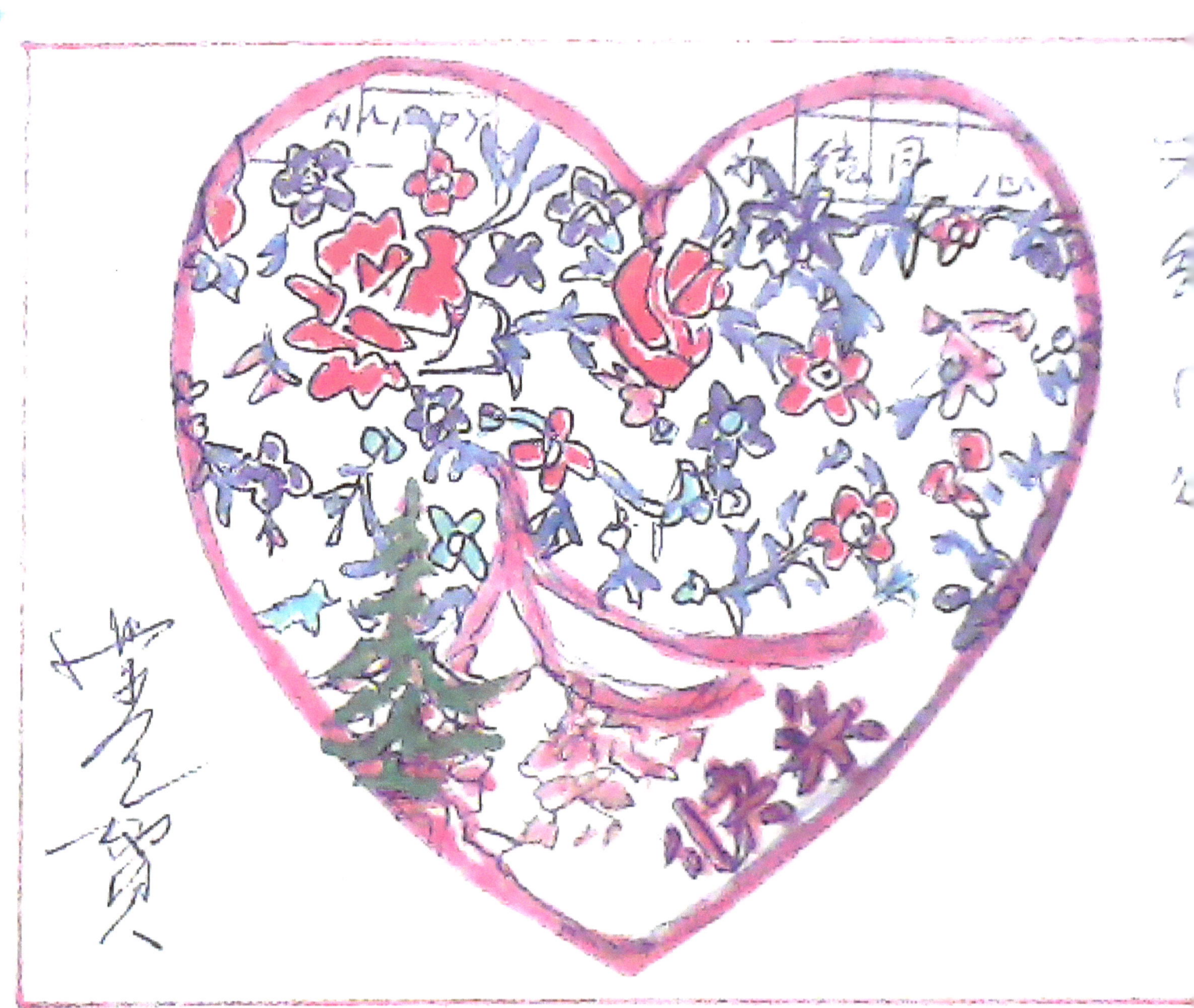

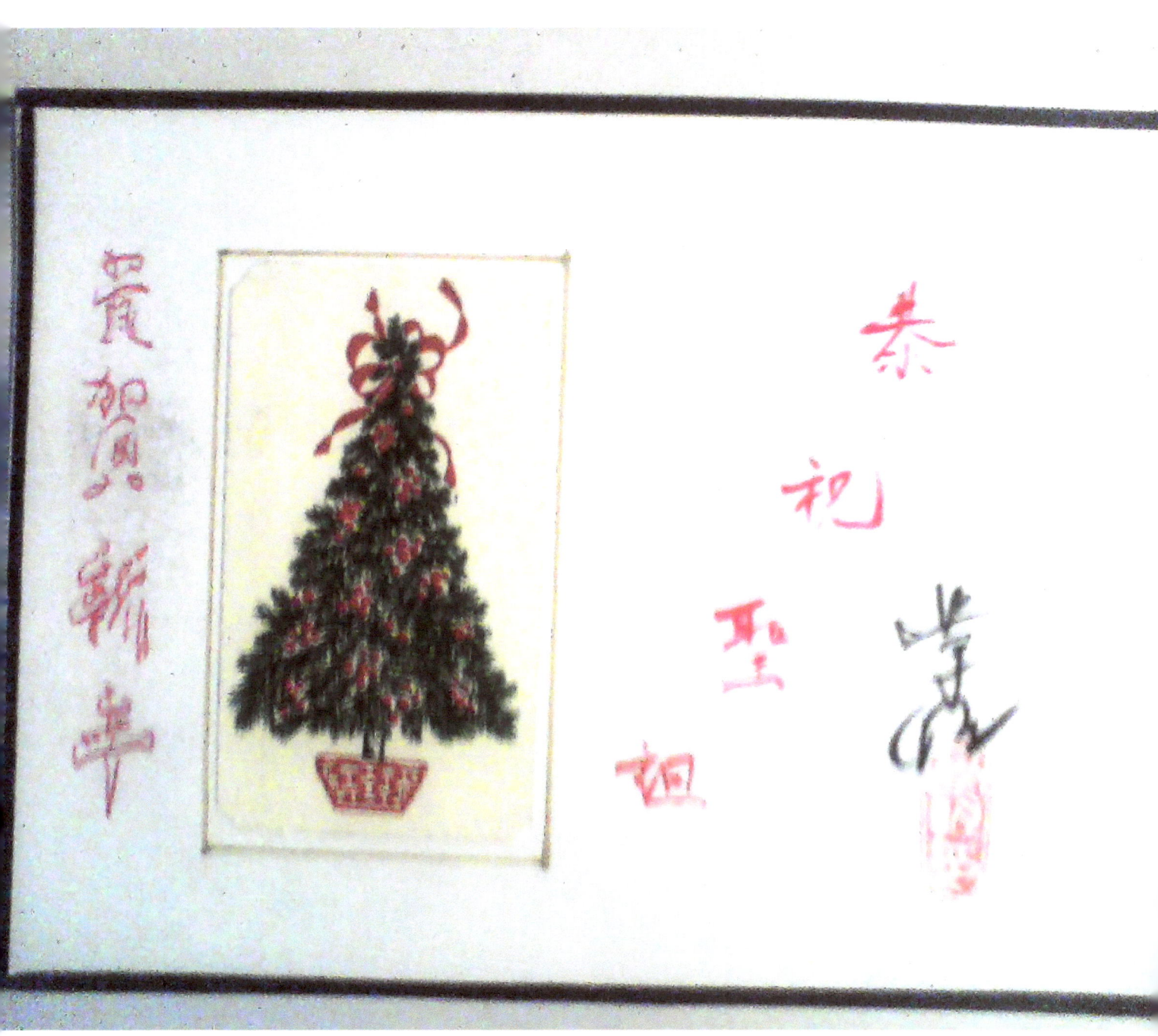

33

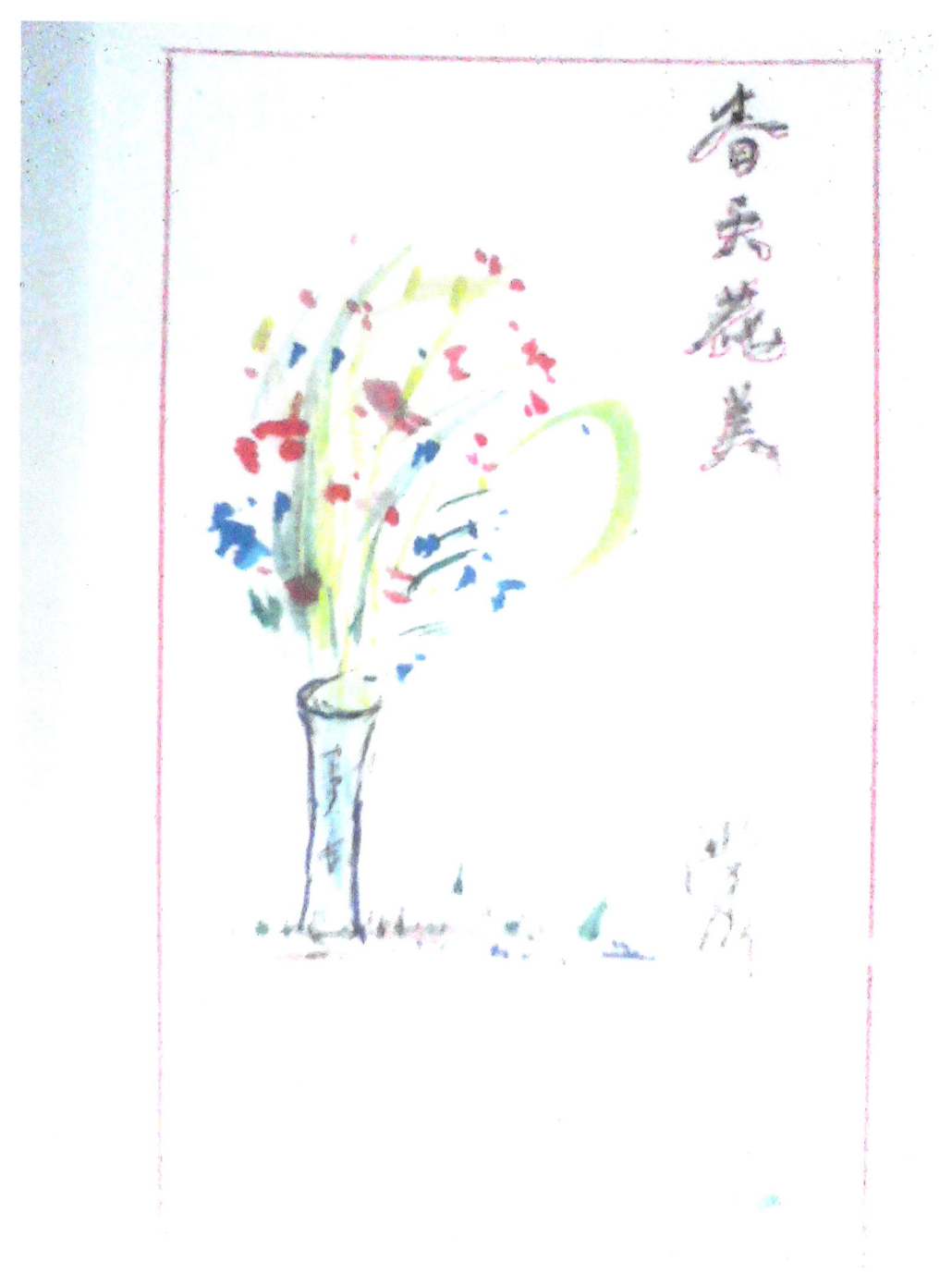

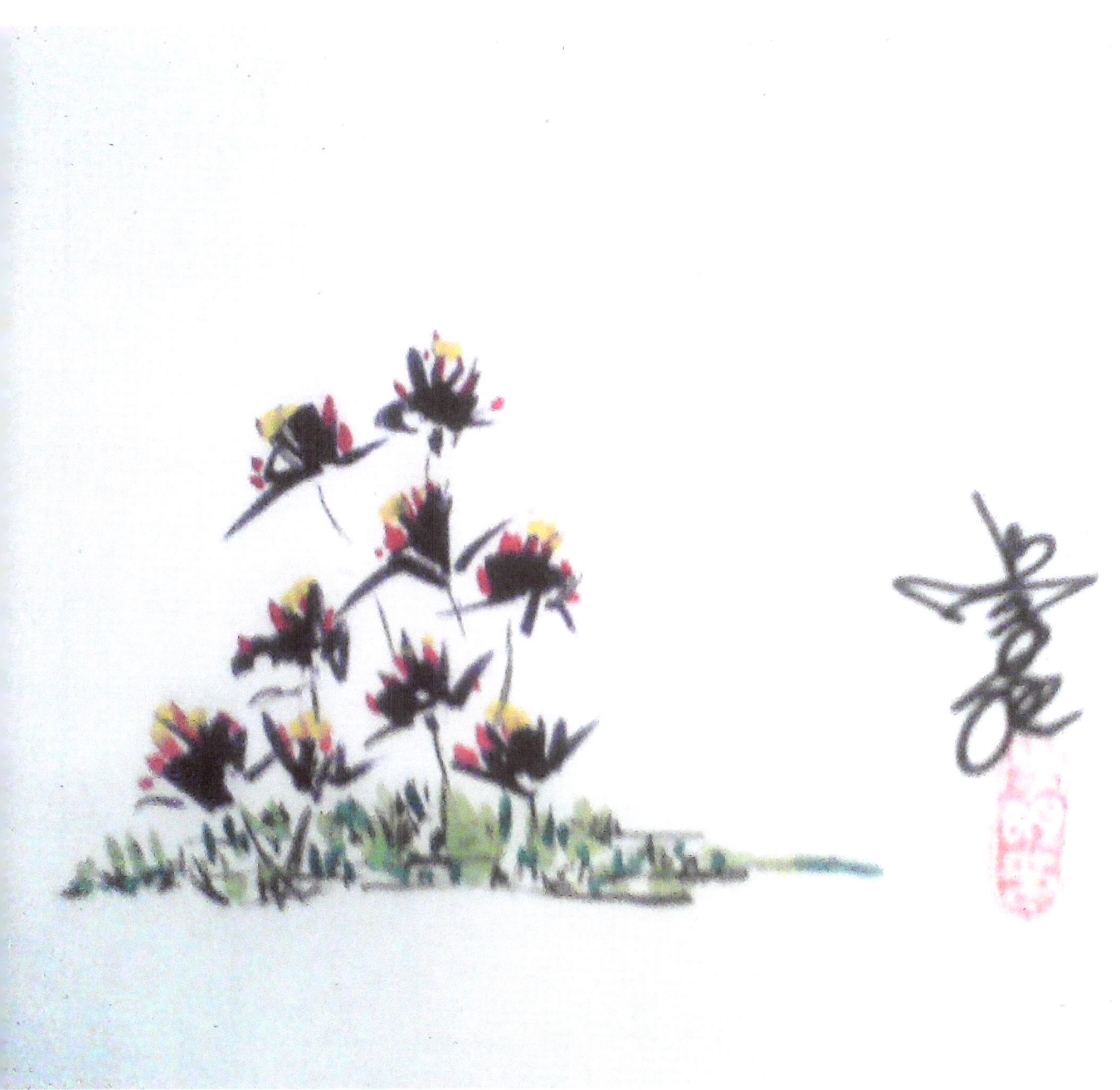

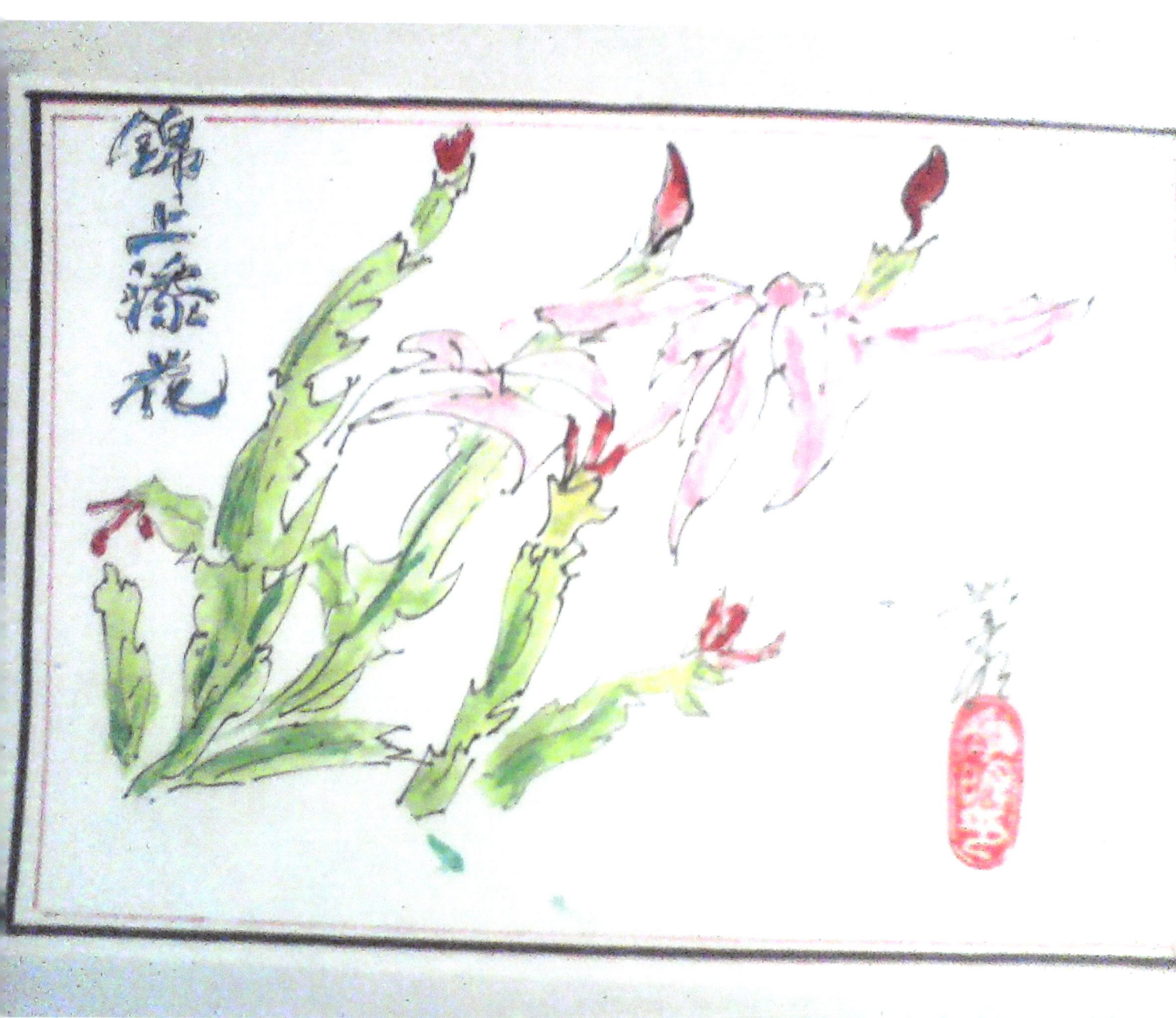

36

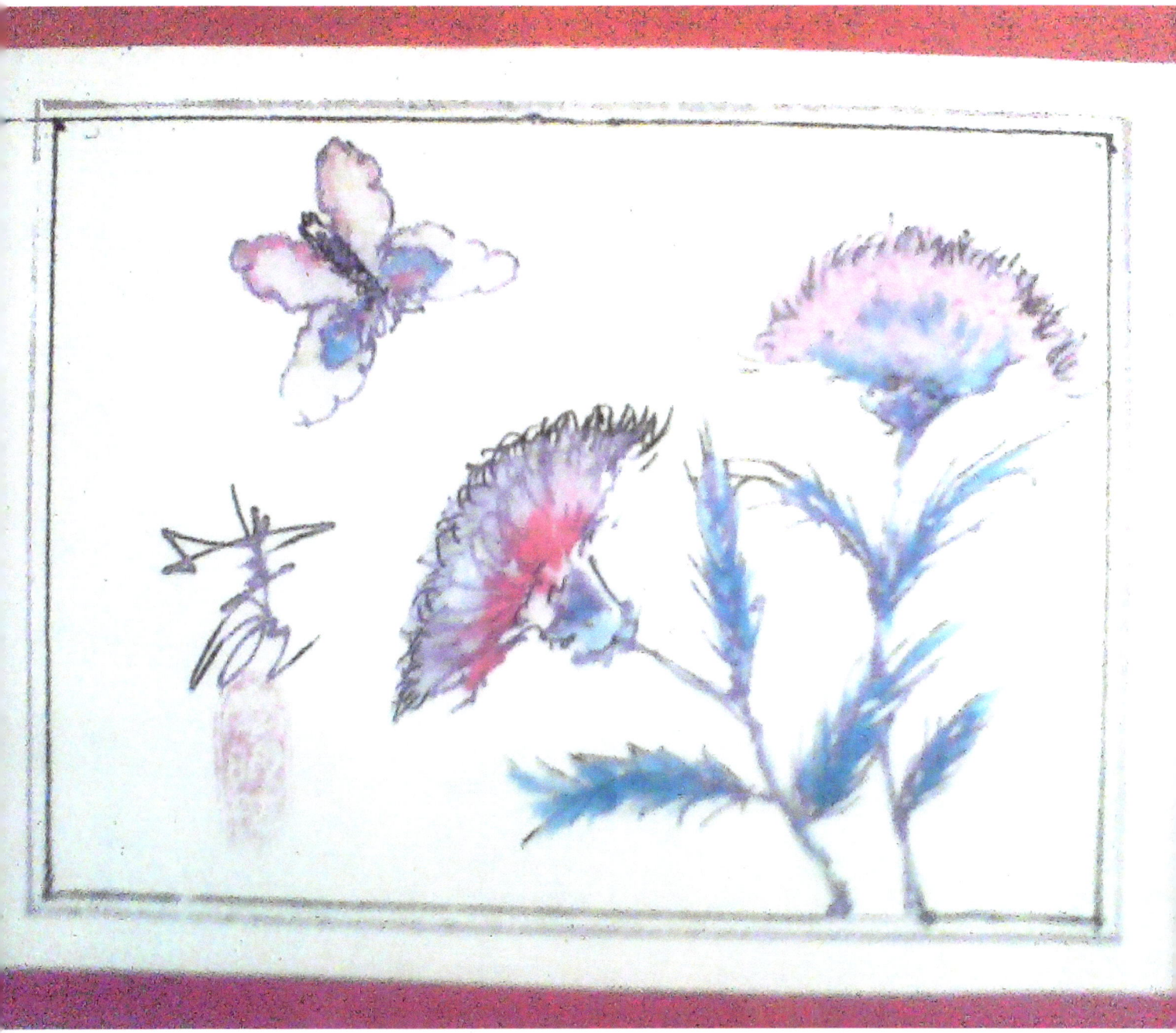

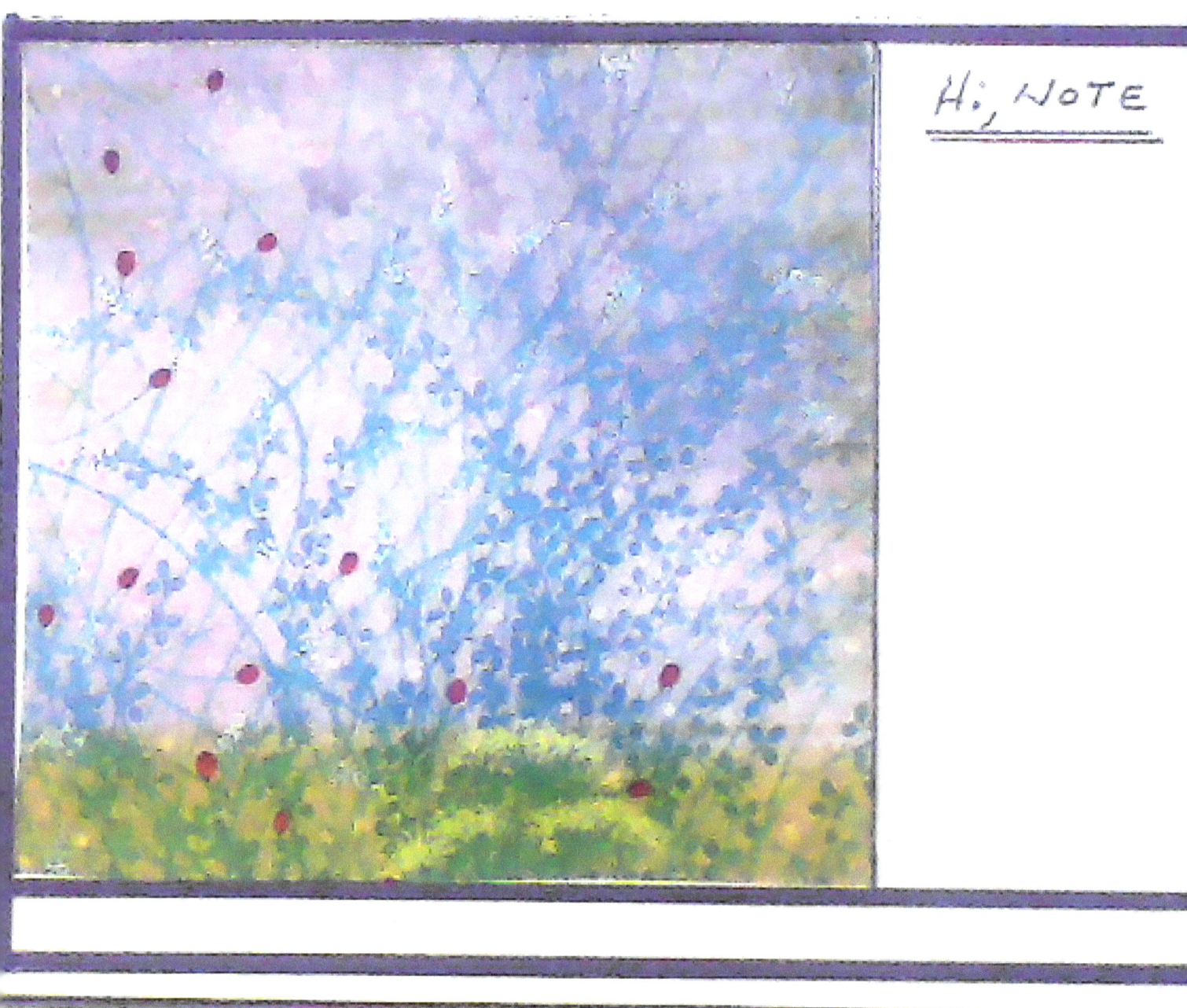

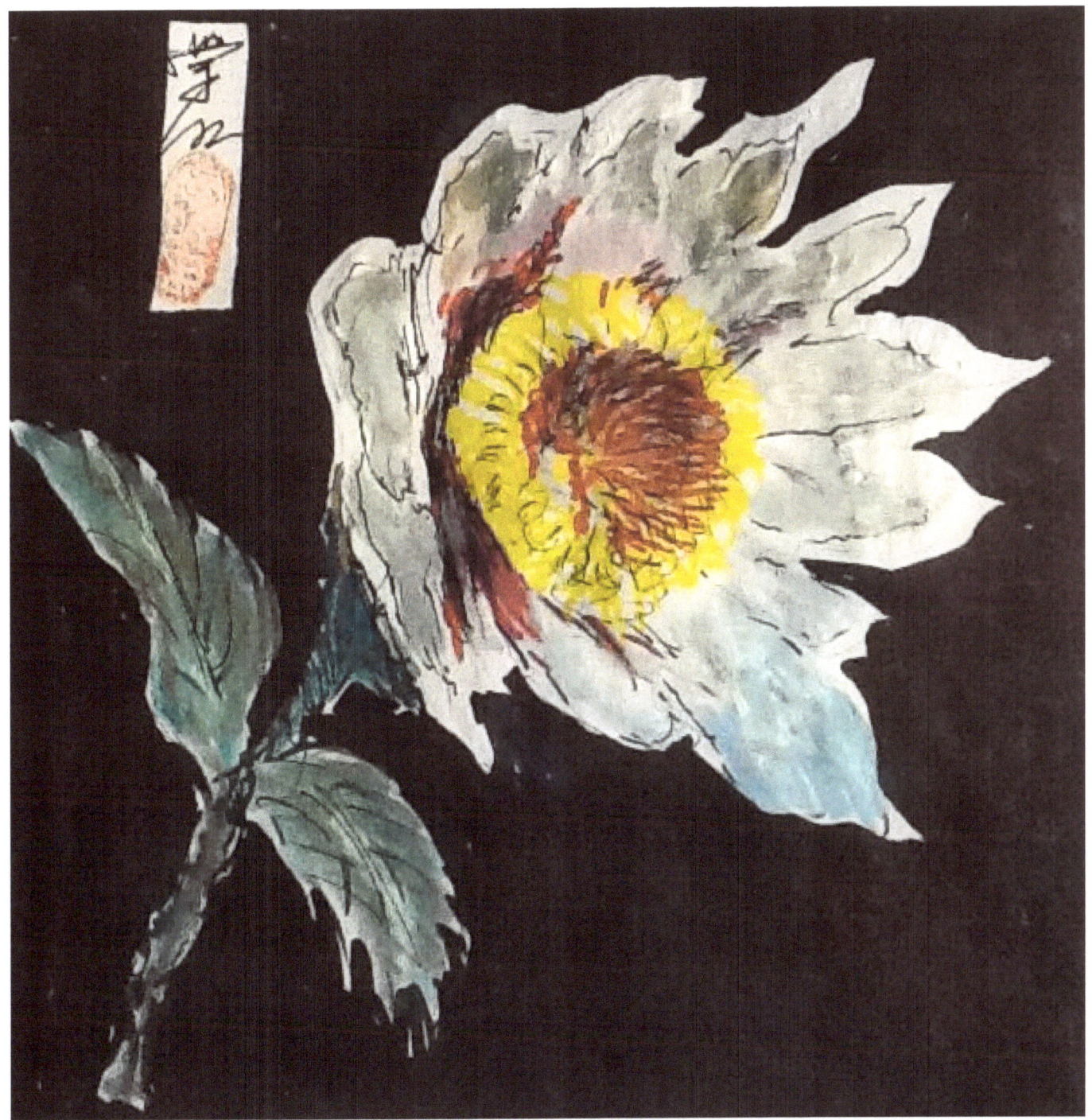

39

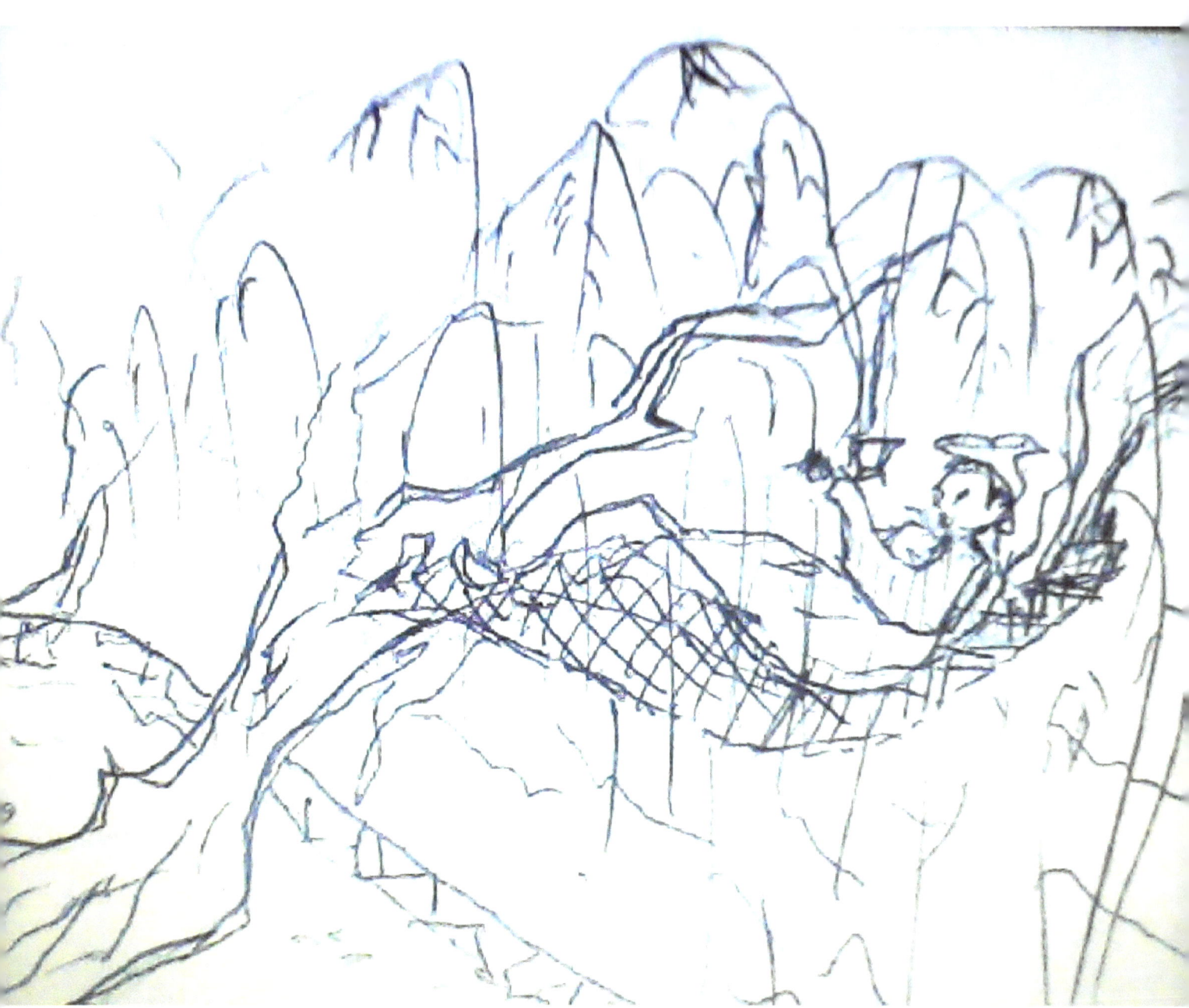

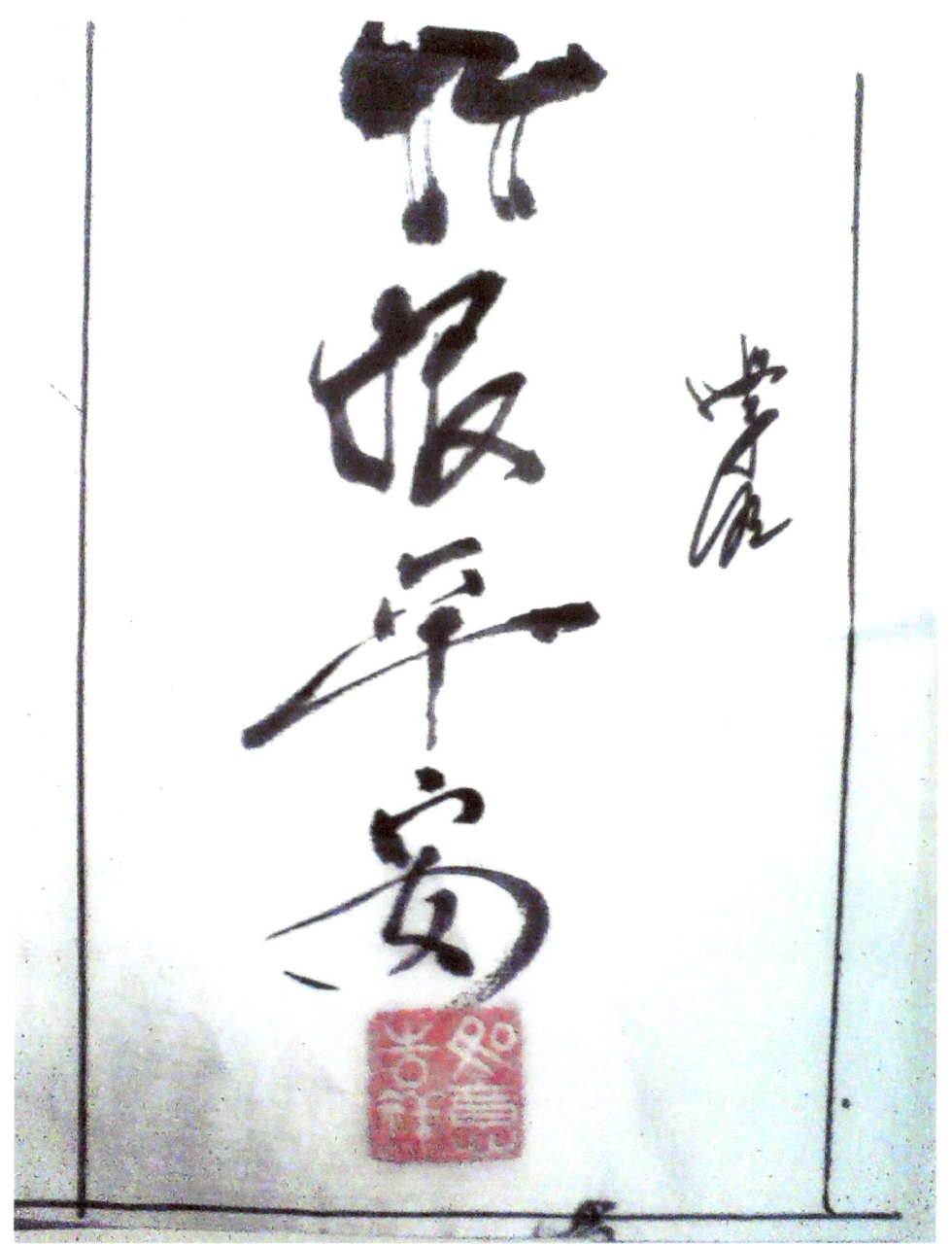

=

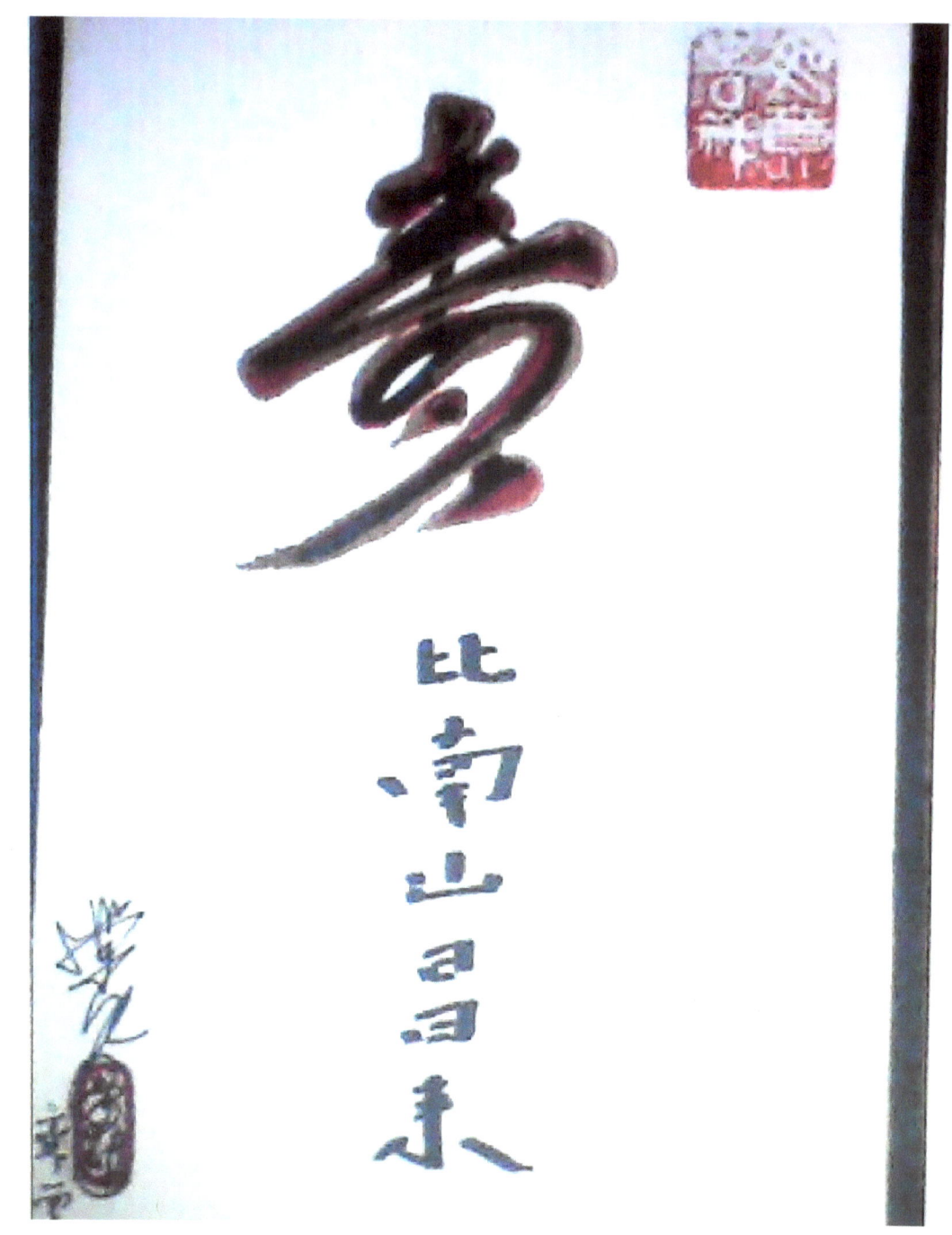

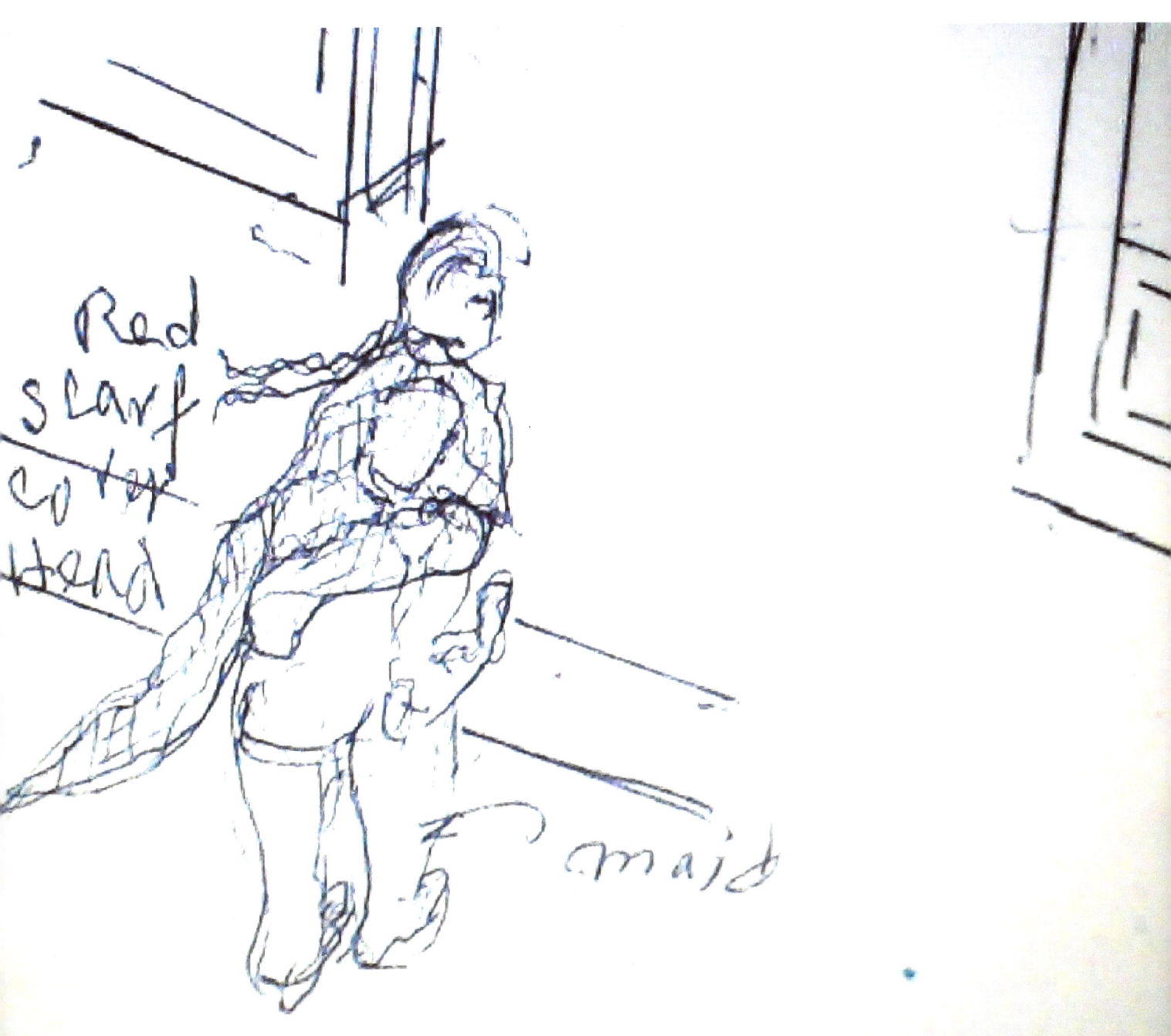

Red
scarf
cover
Head

E maid

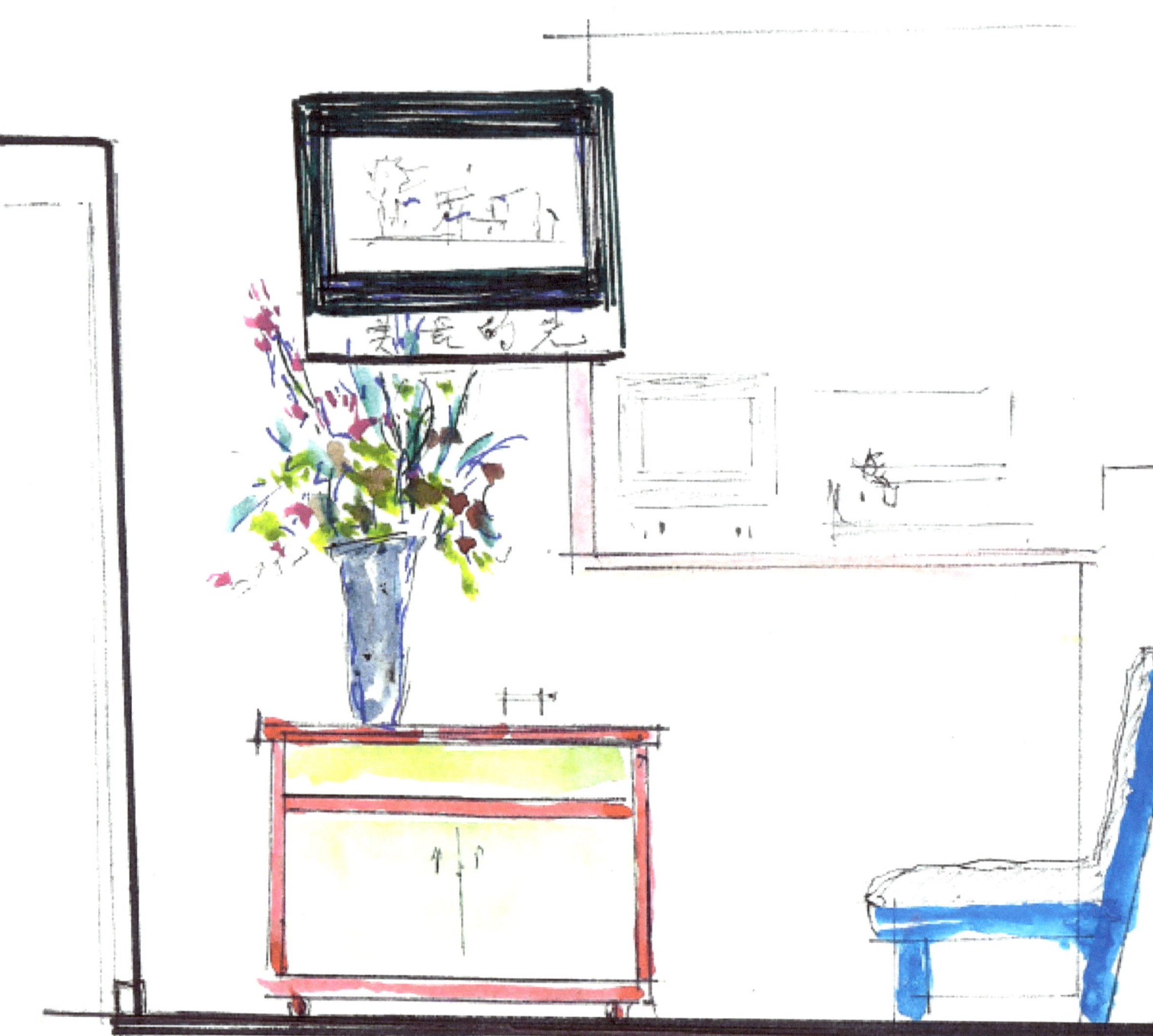

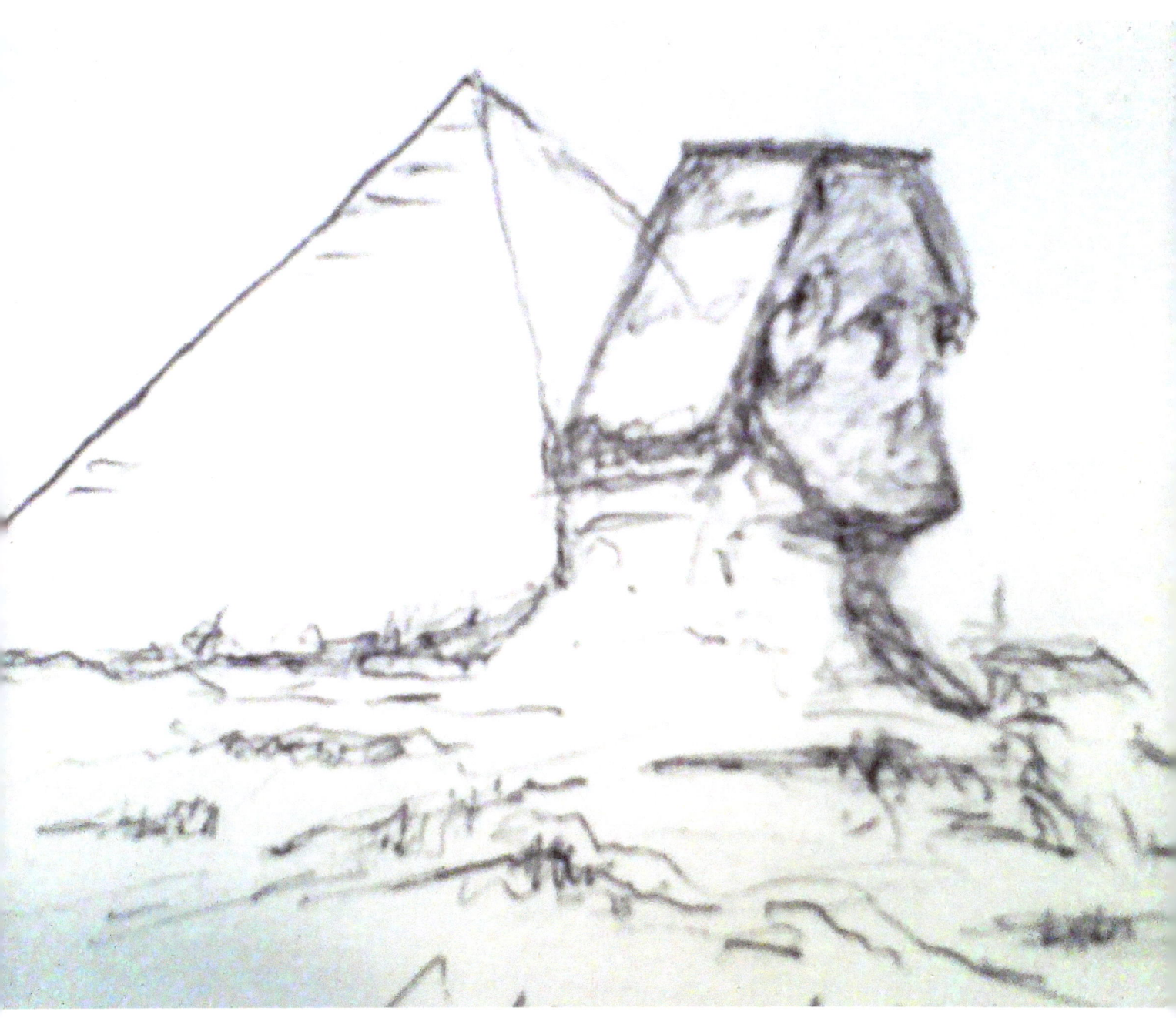

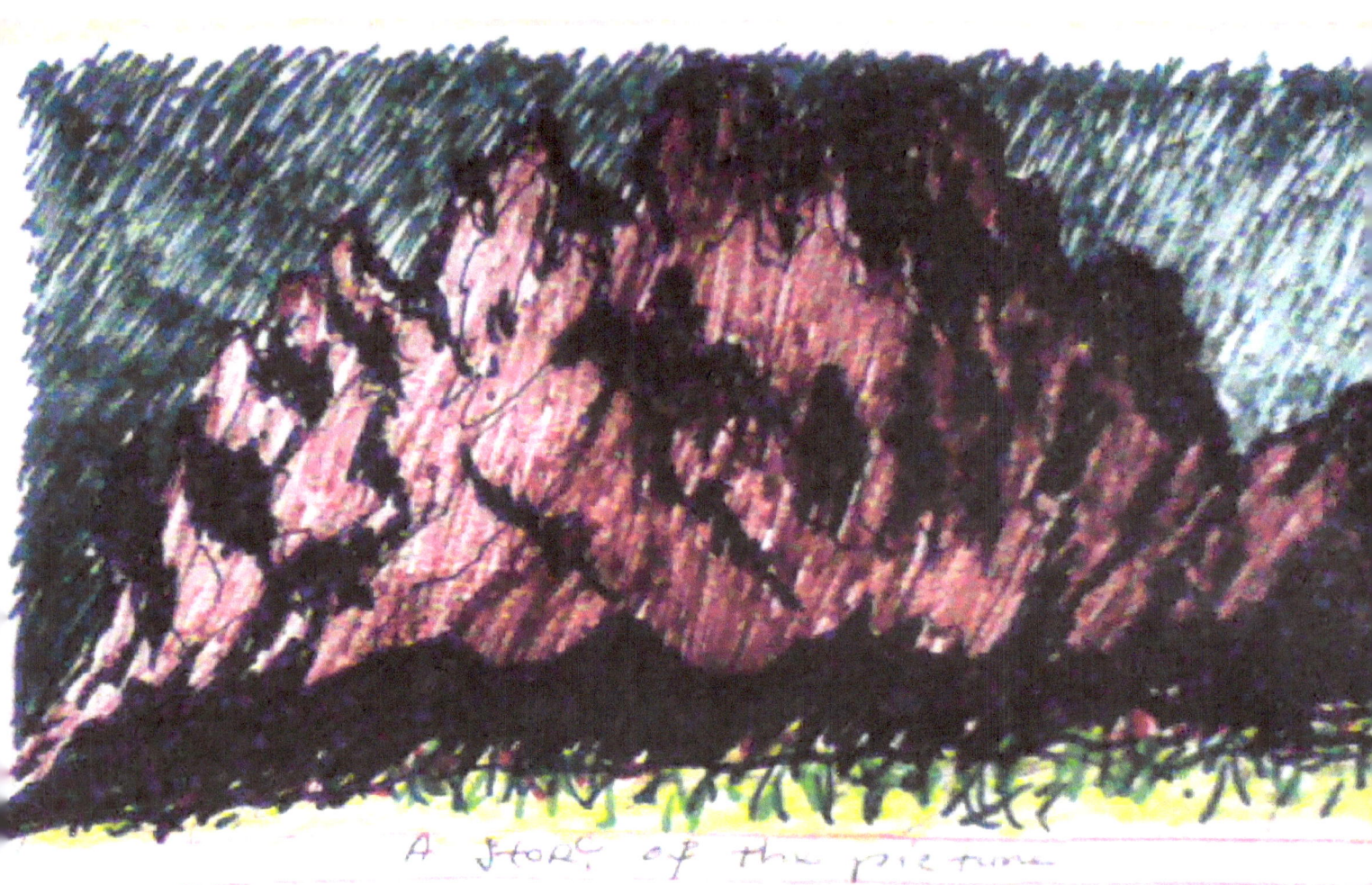

A Story of the picture

One of the Story of a Canadian Mt. The Indian chief was
the daughter of this marry this Guy then will tell him w
the Gold hiding place. this Guy promised to MARRY HER
soon AS the chief told him the location, He change his m
Not to MARRY His daughter the chief said mad. Cur
the Town All the prosperity was gone, more than a

46

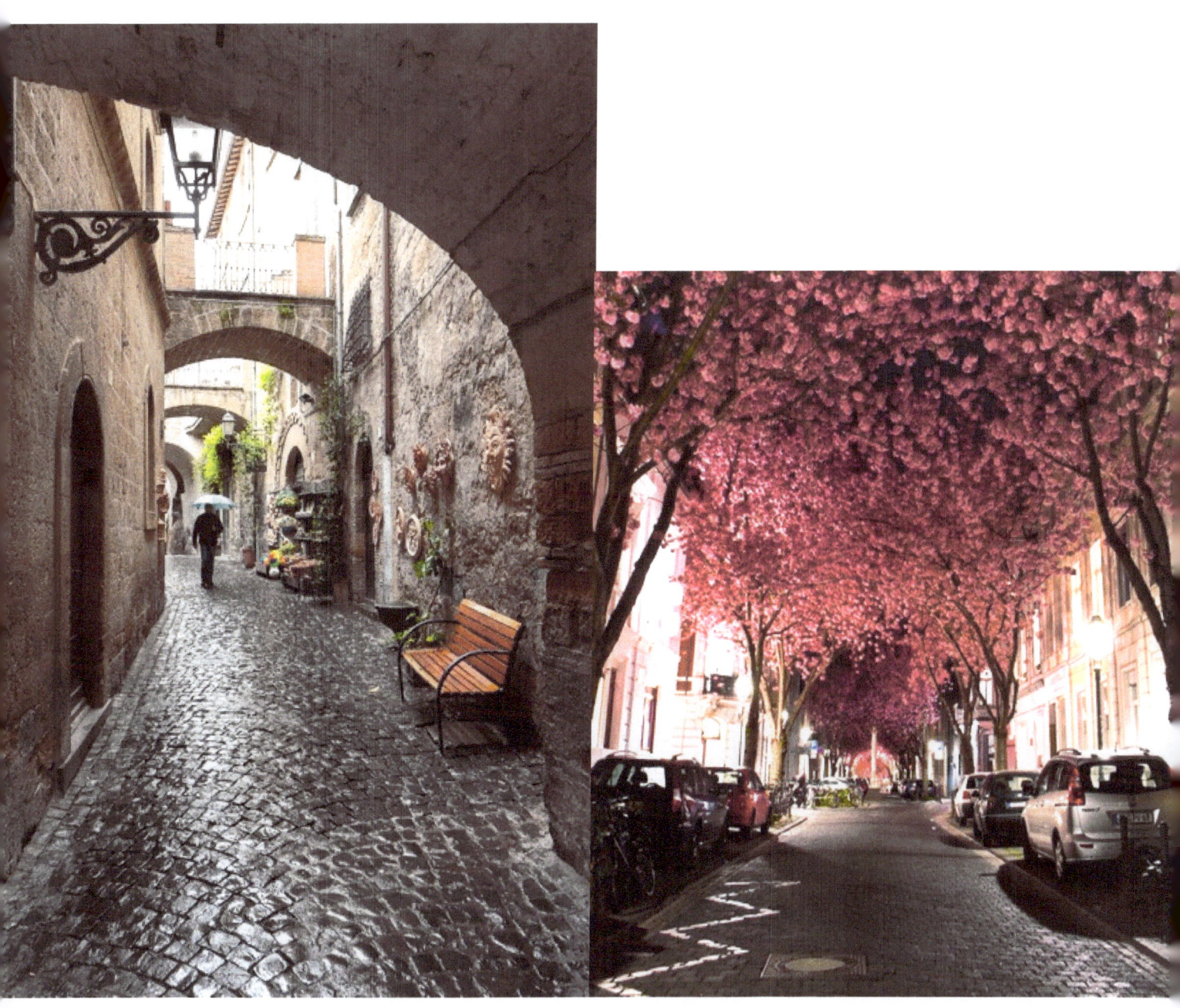

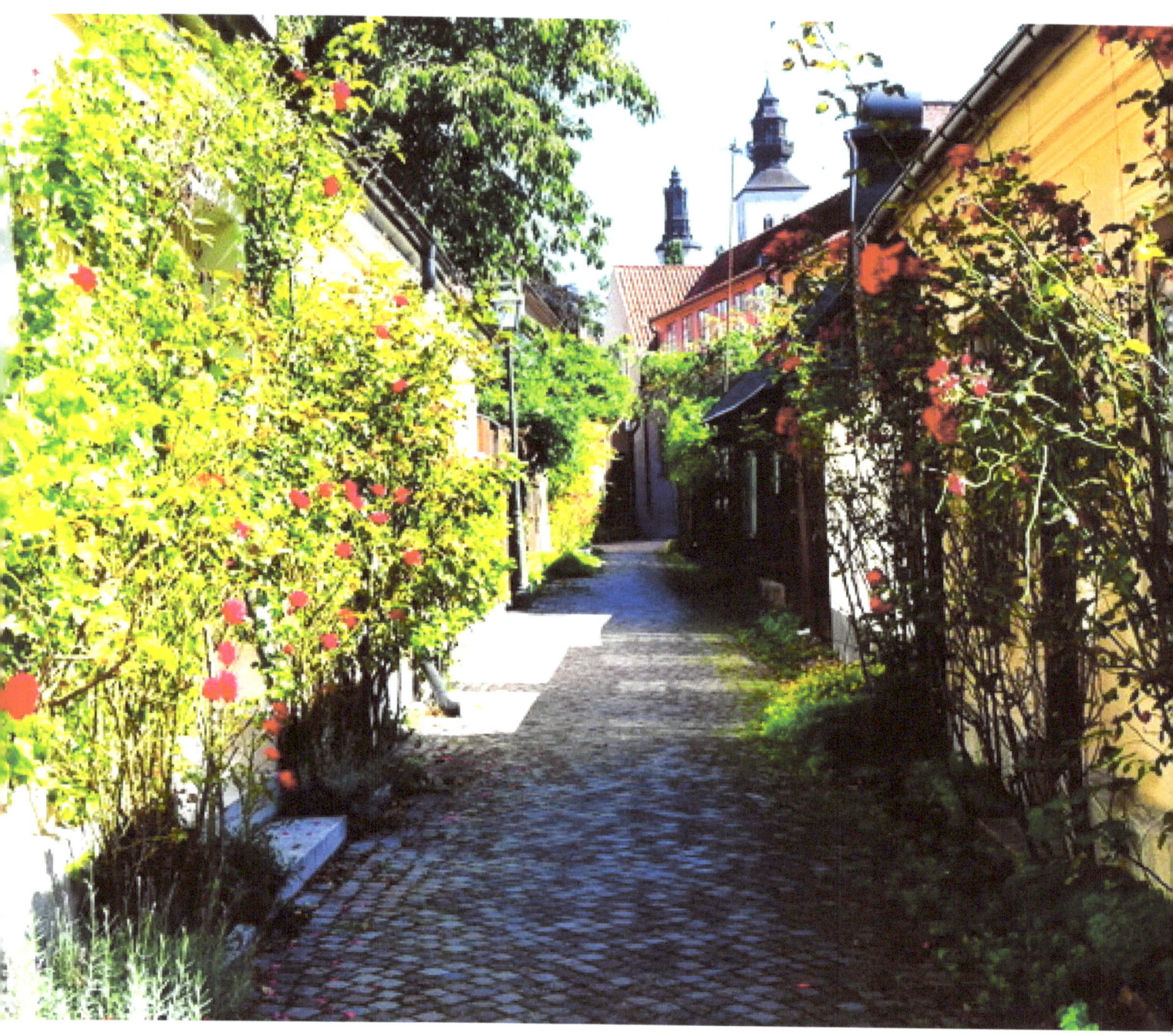

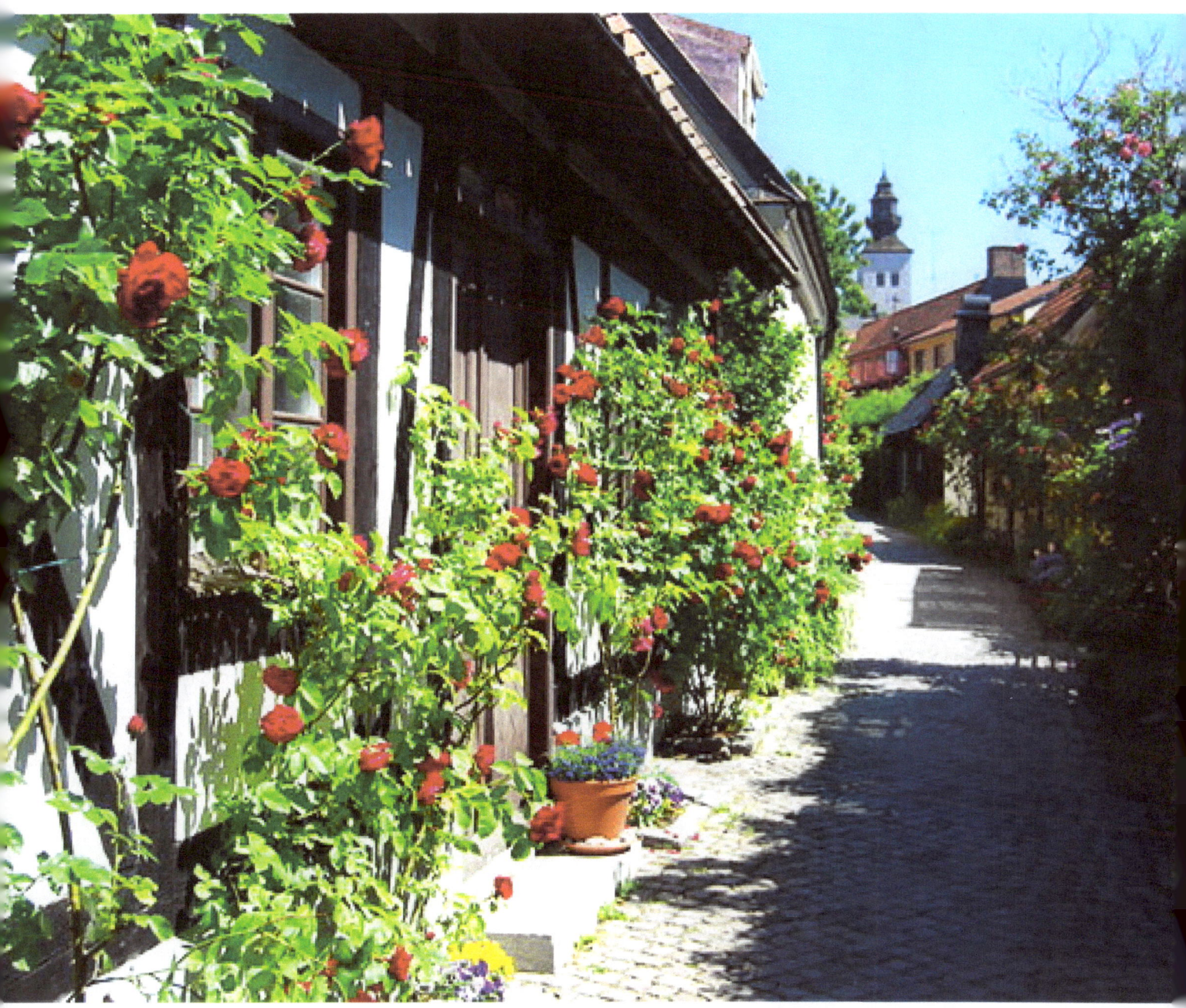

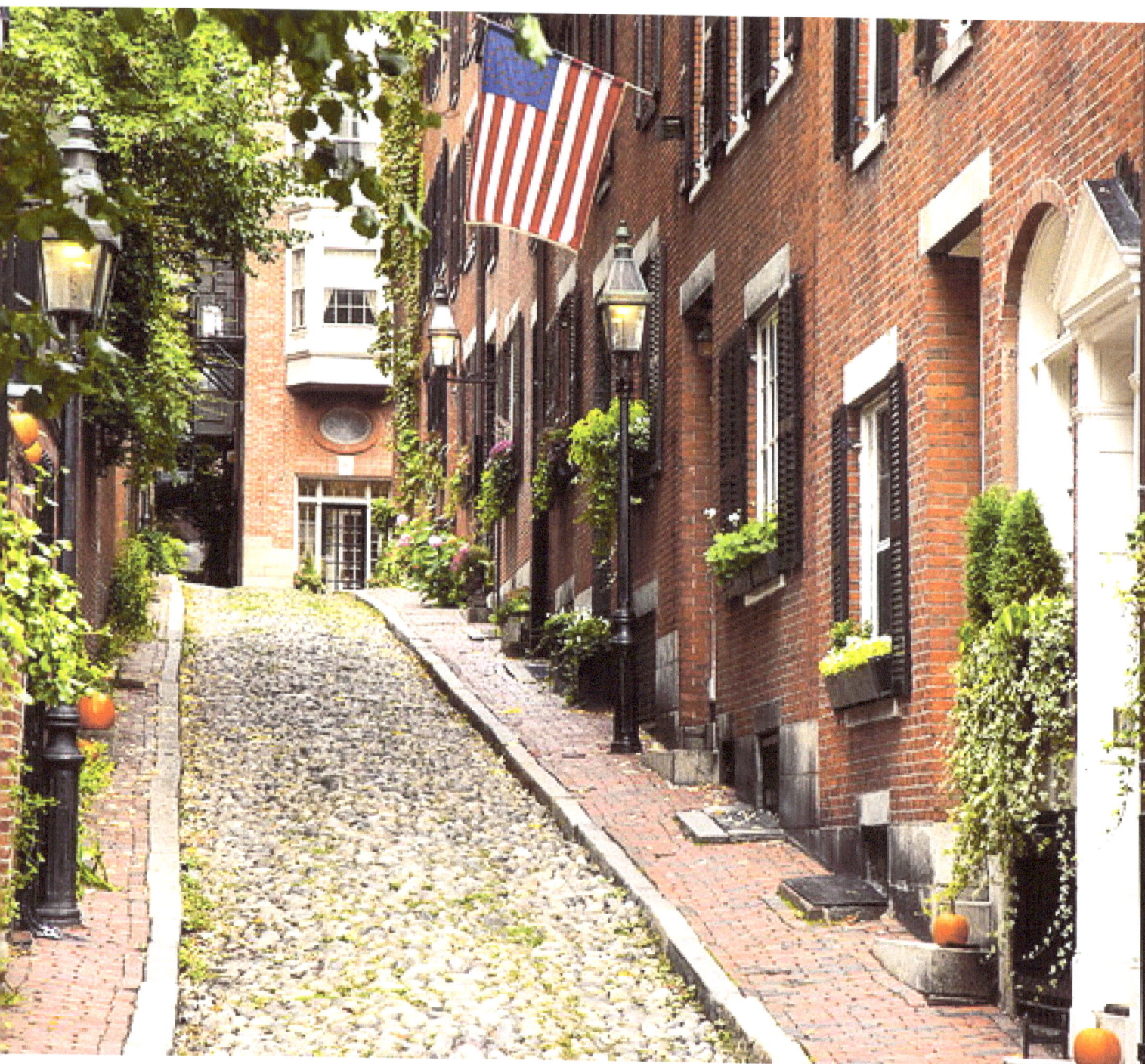

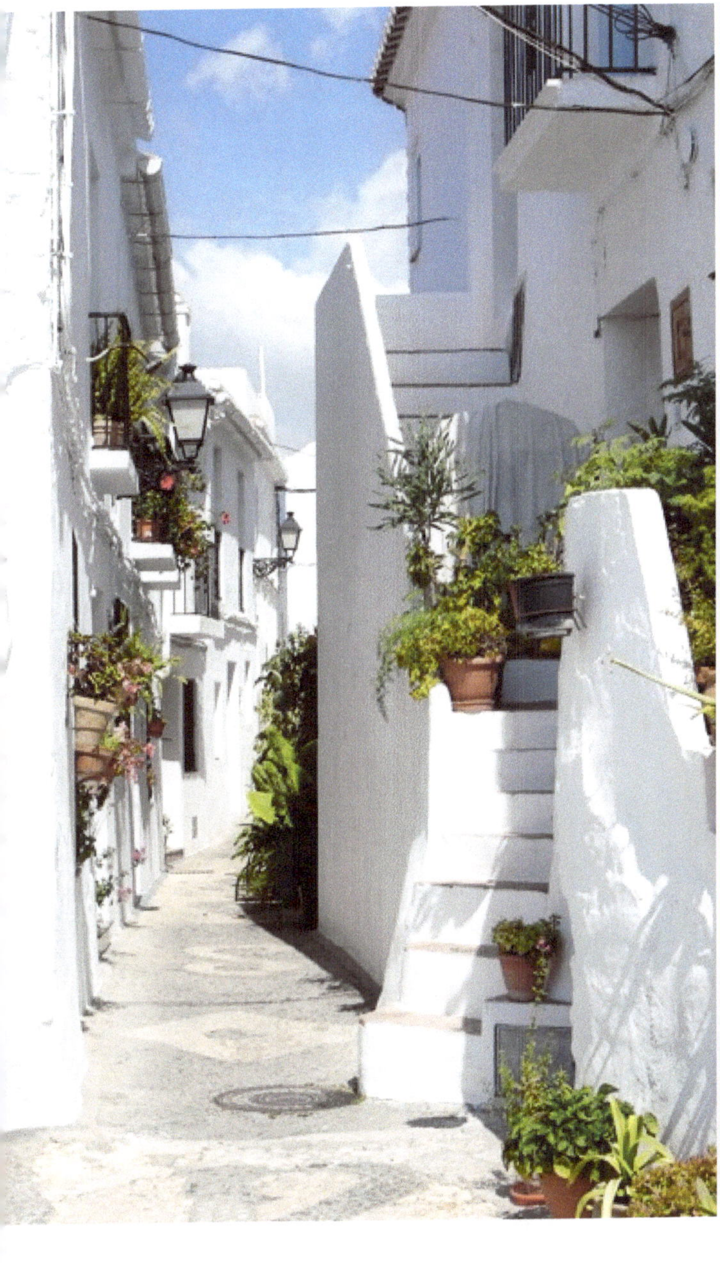

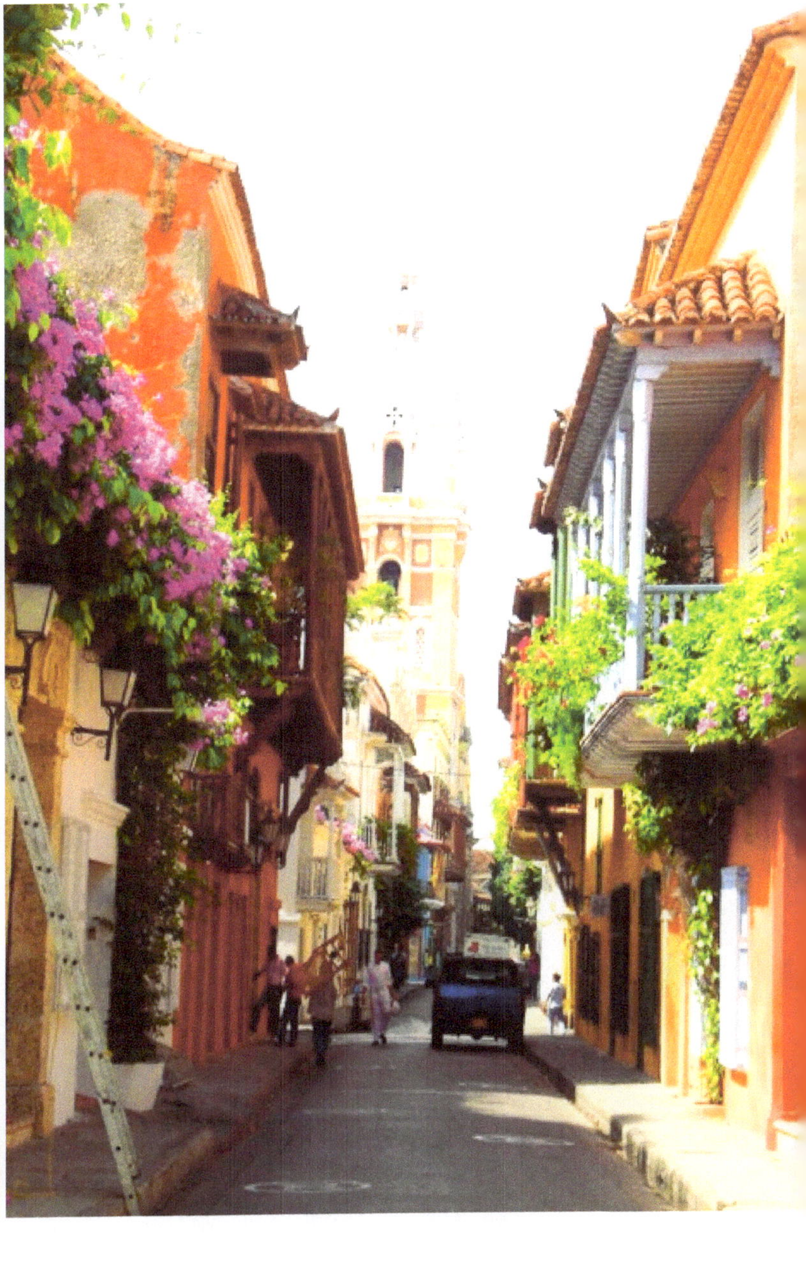

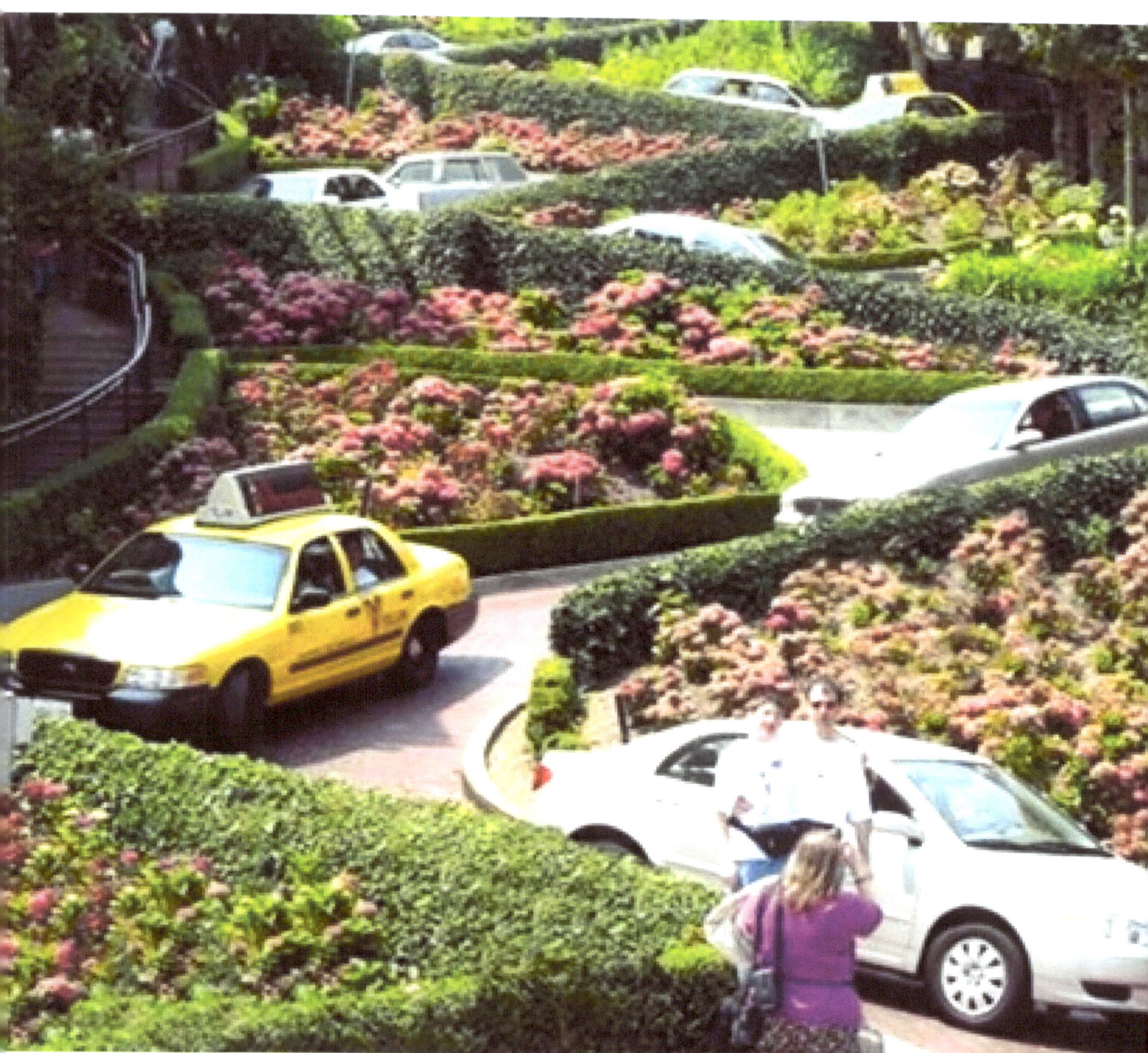

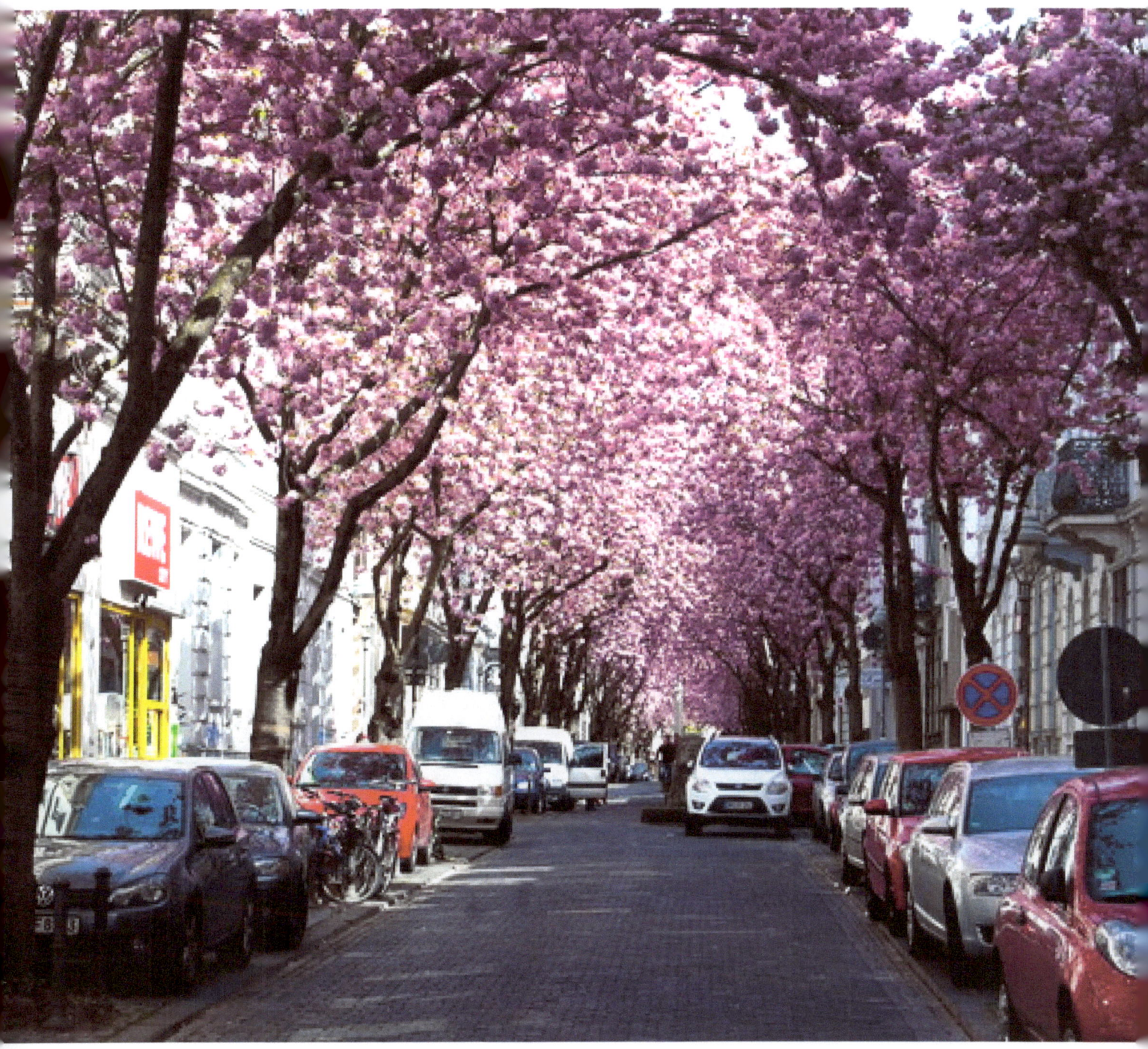

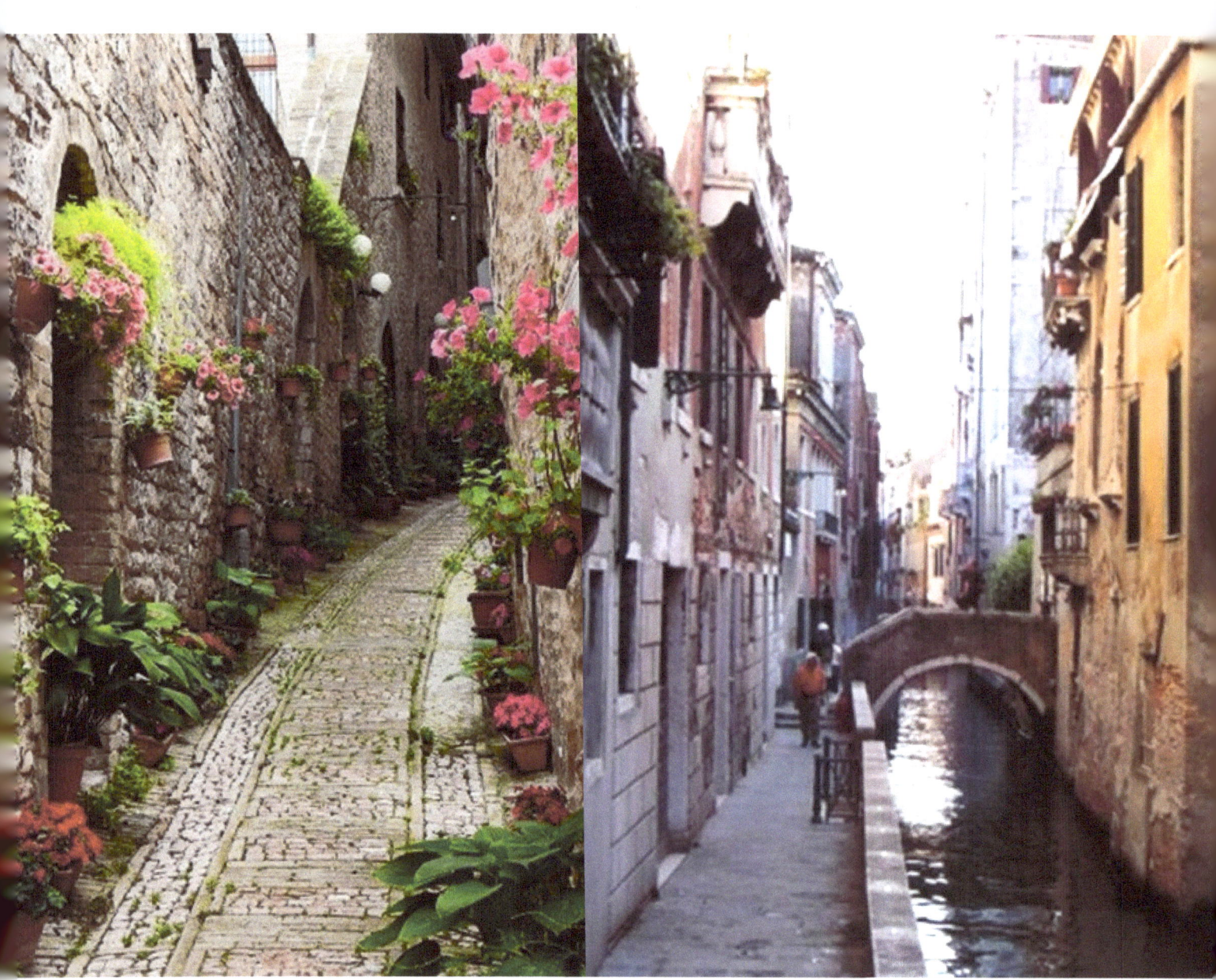

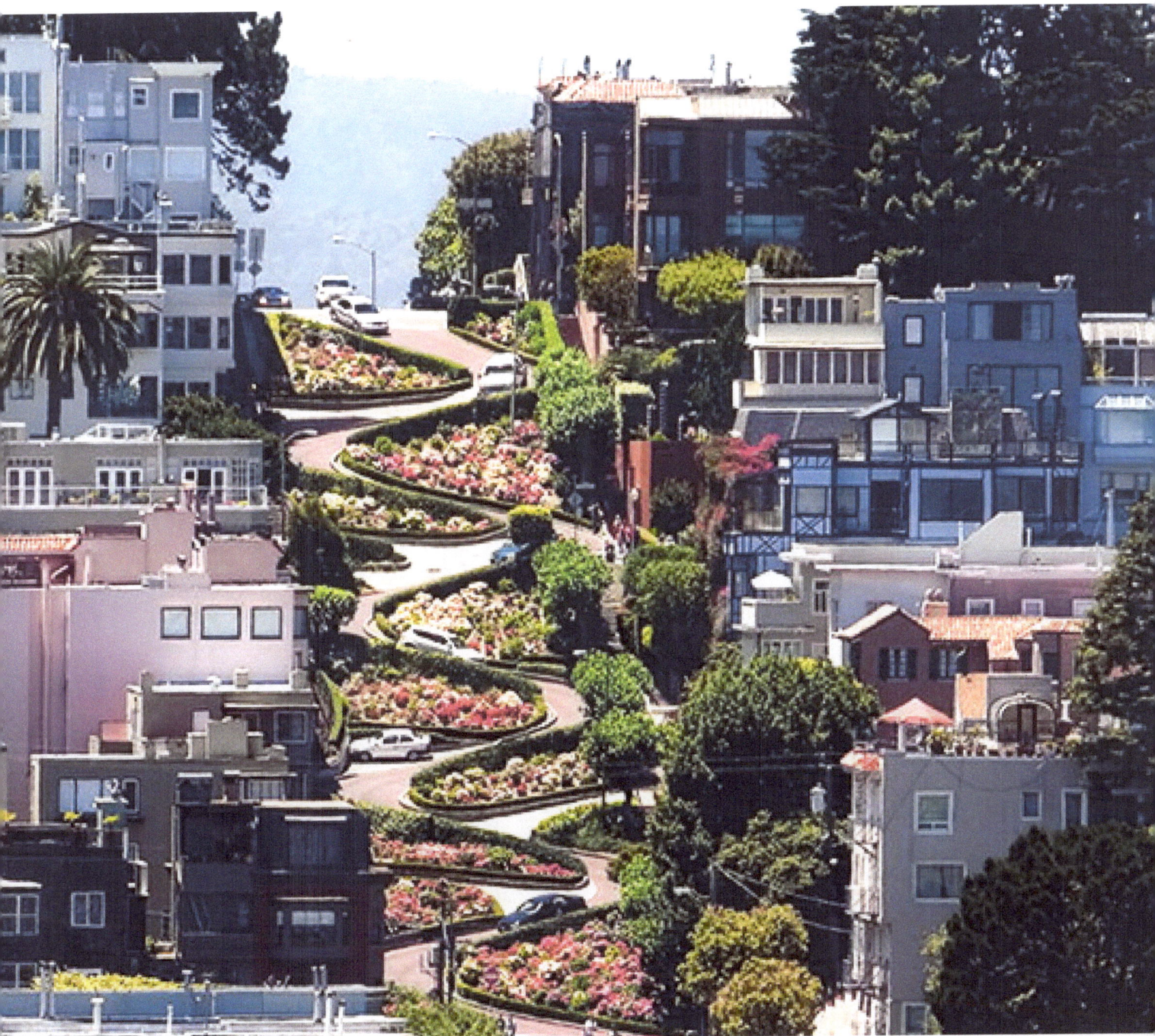

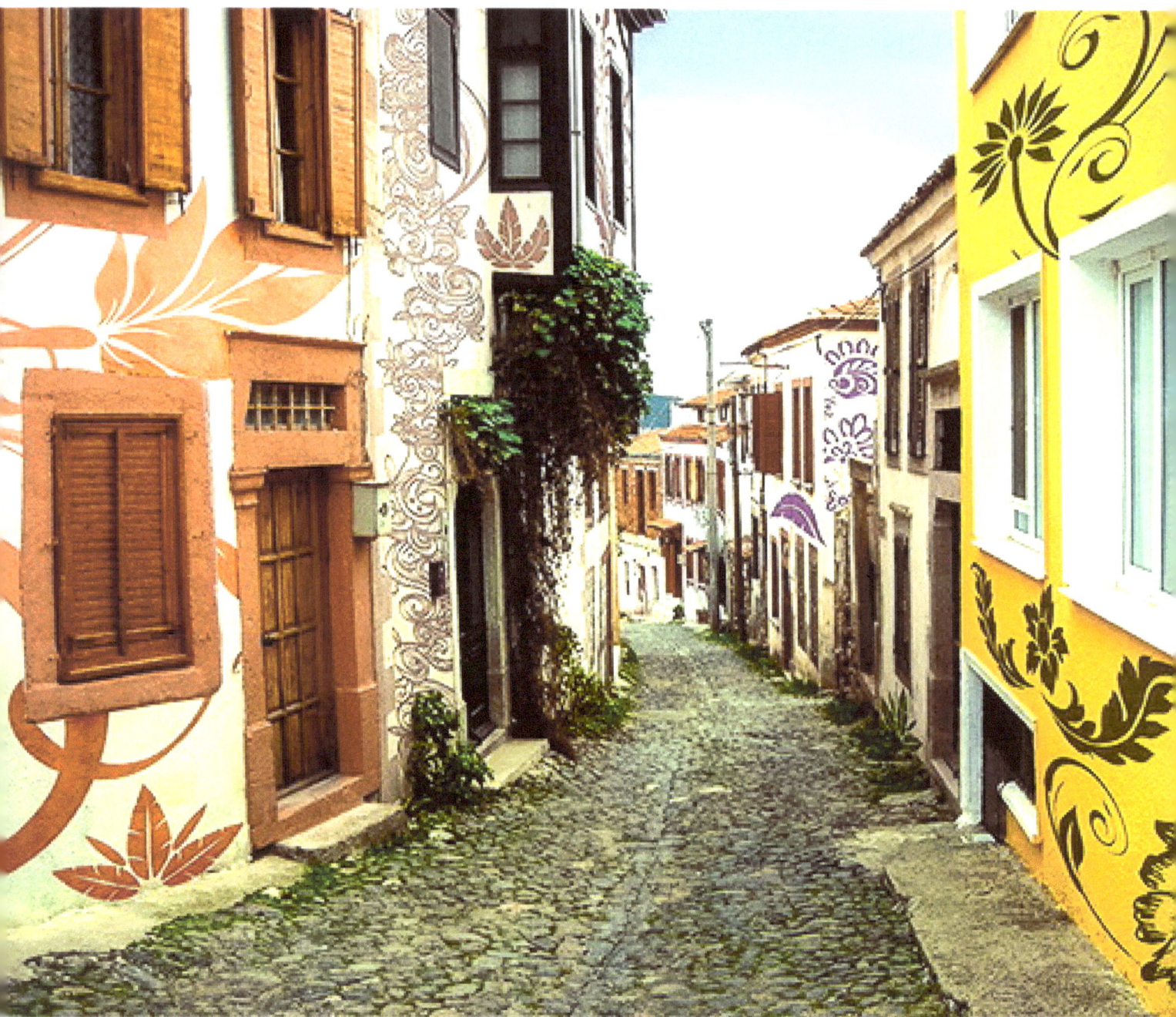

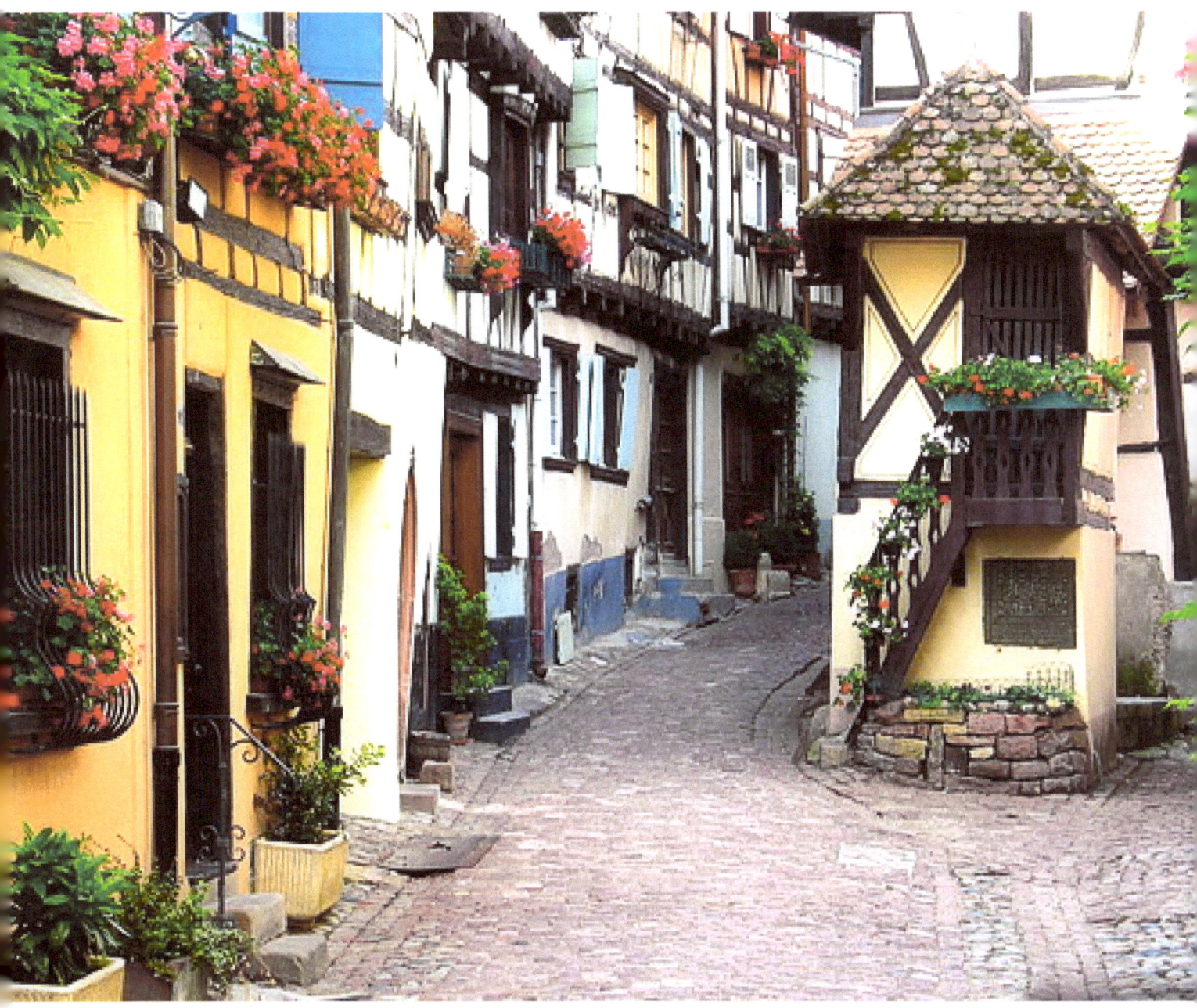

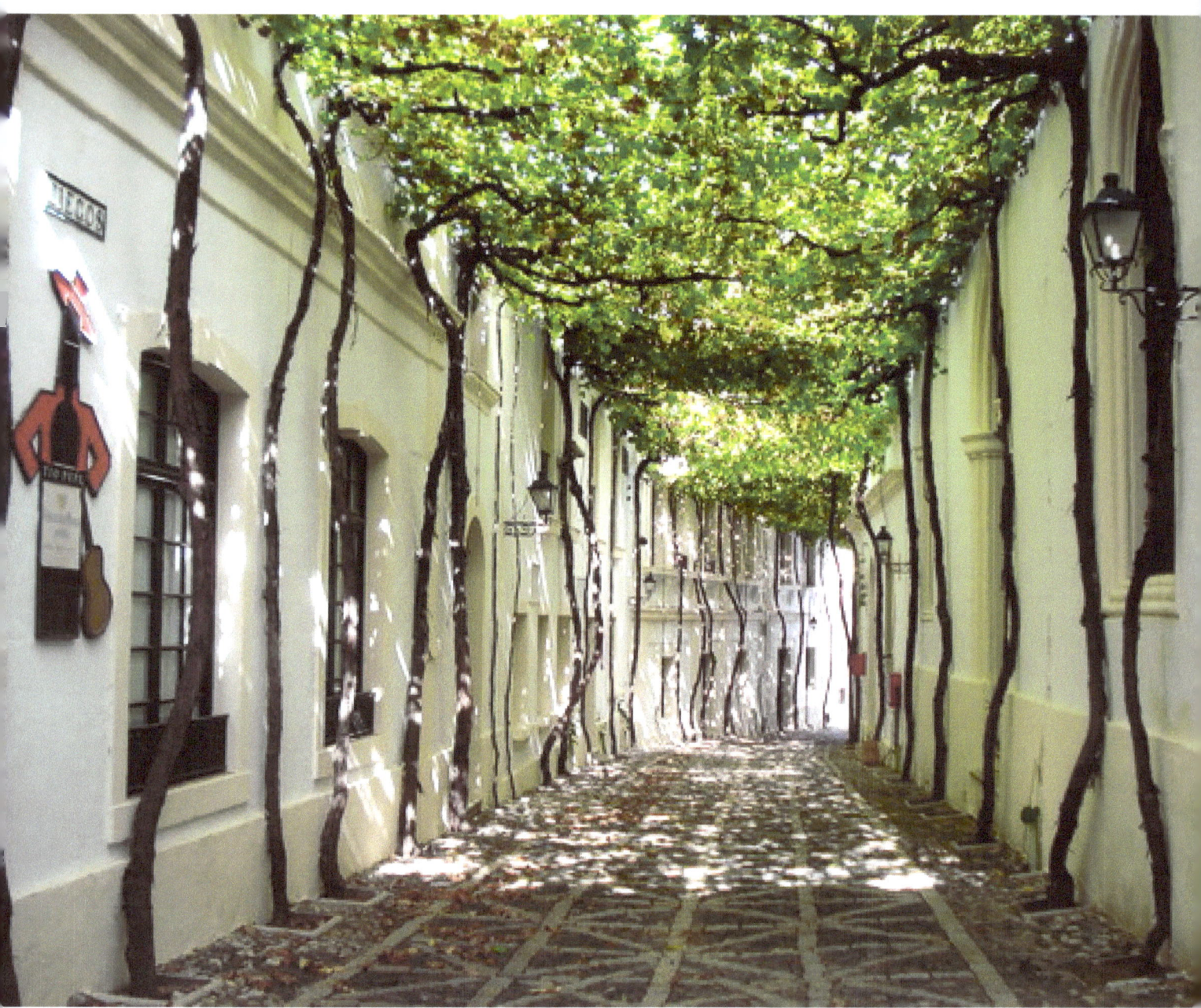

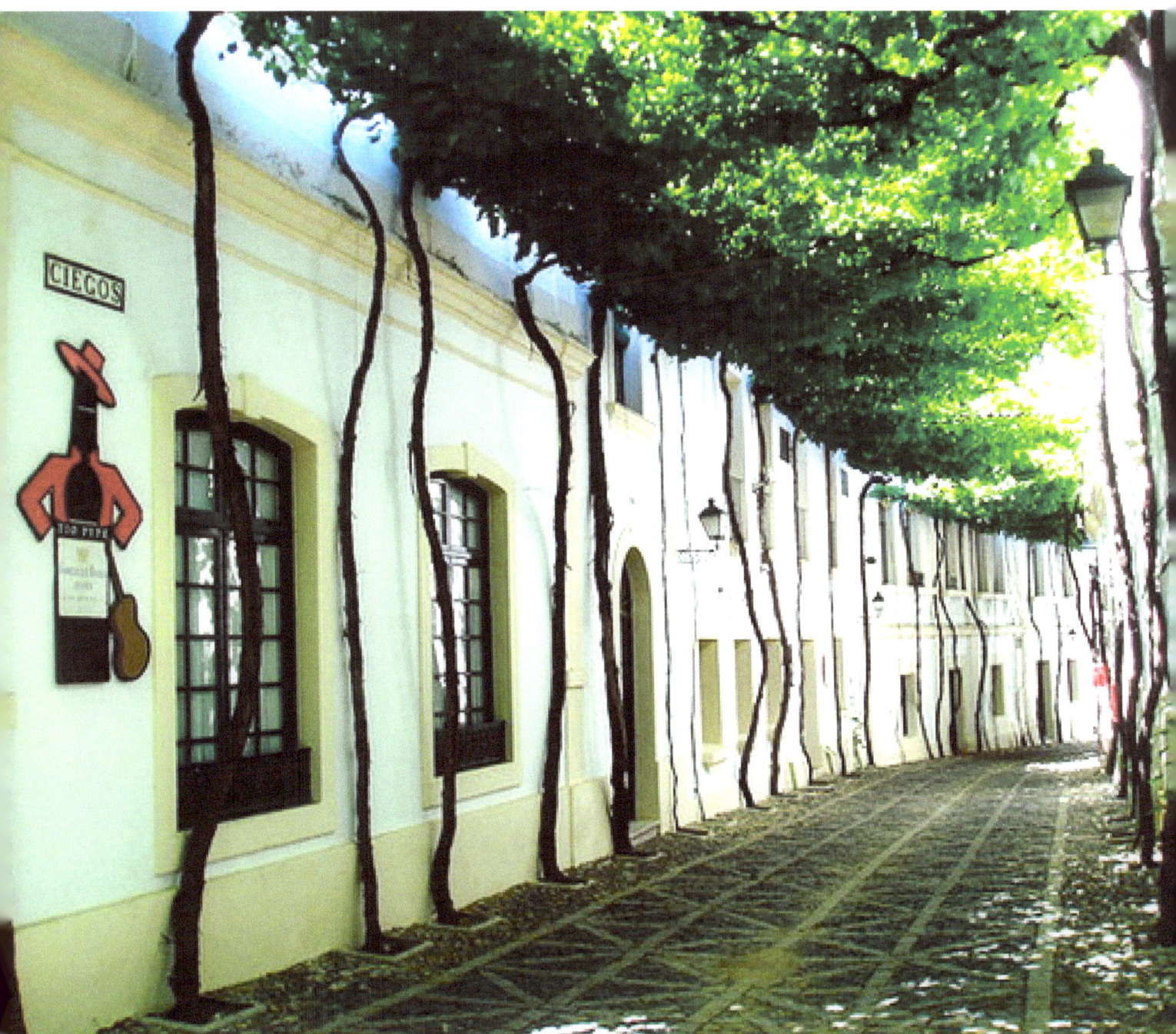

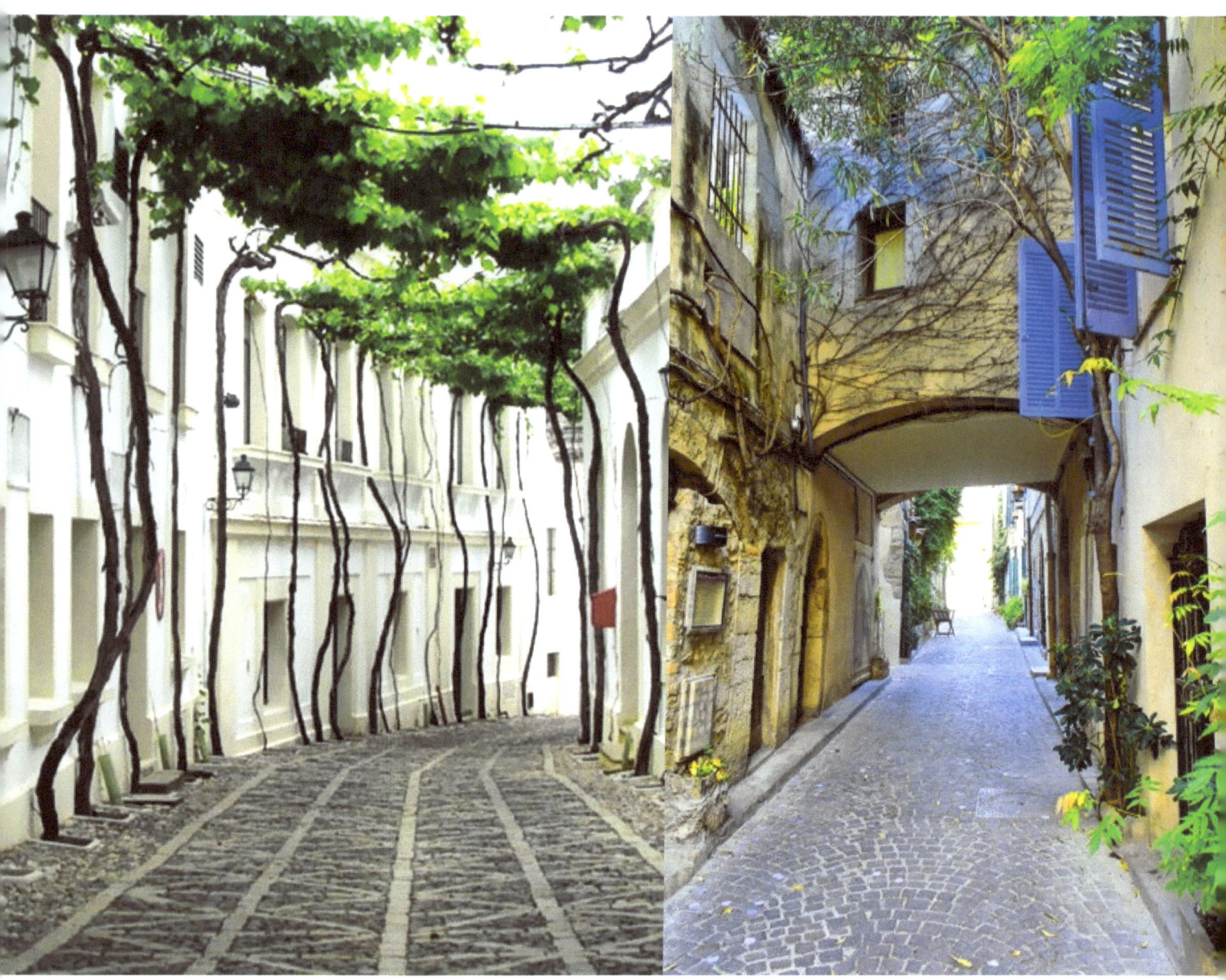

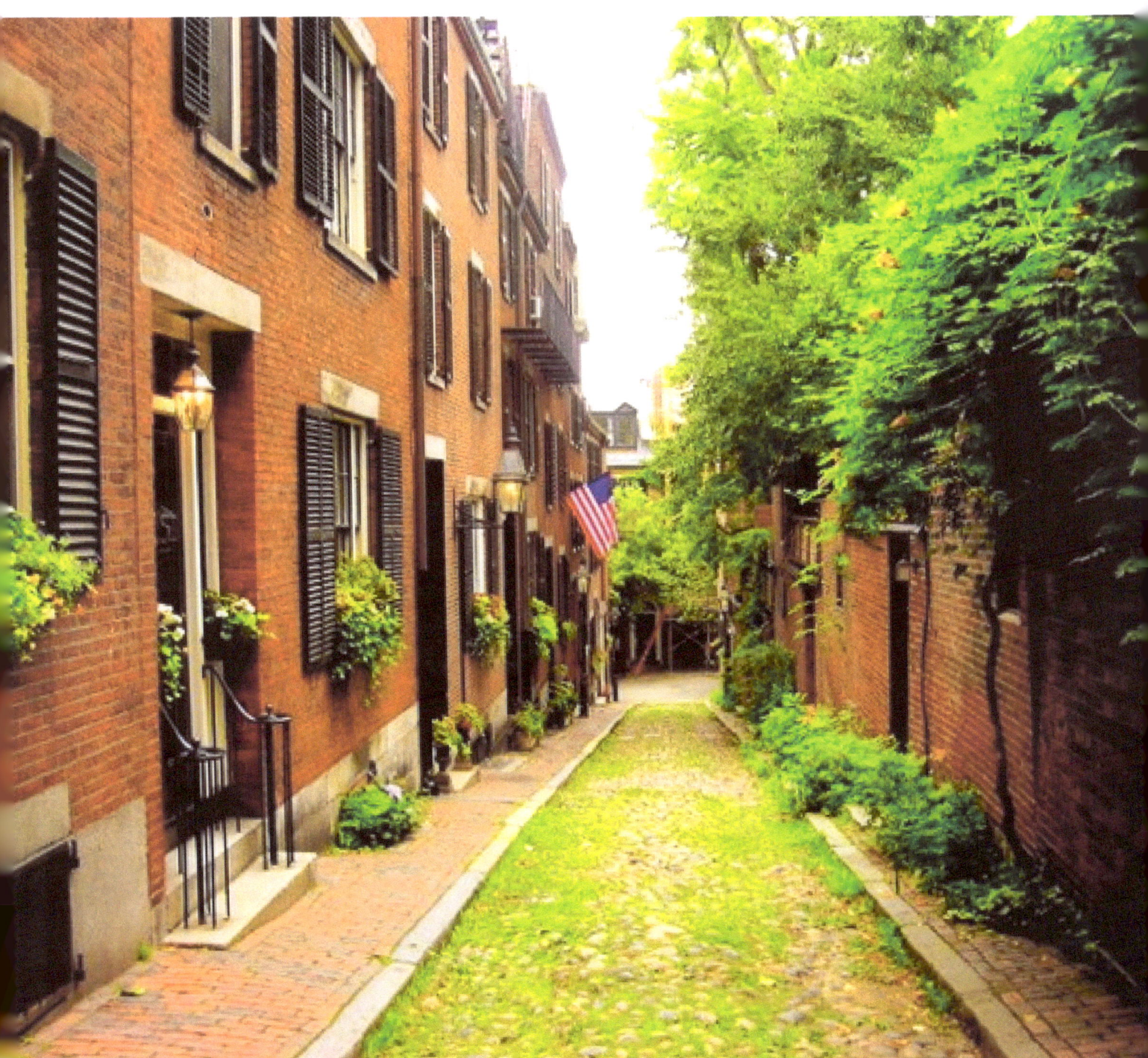

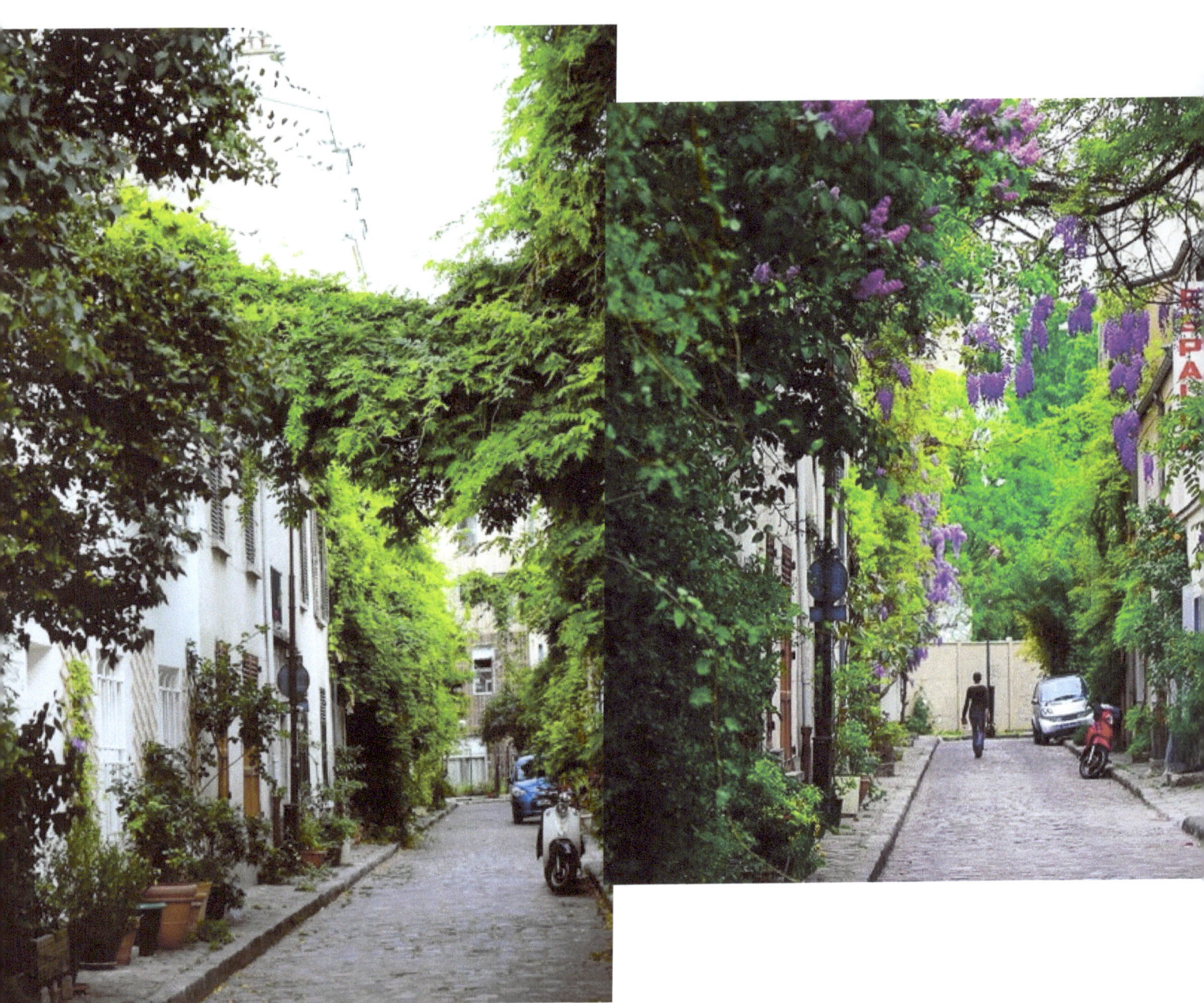

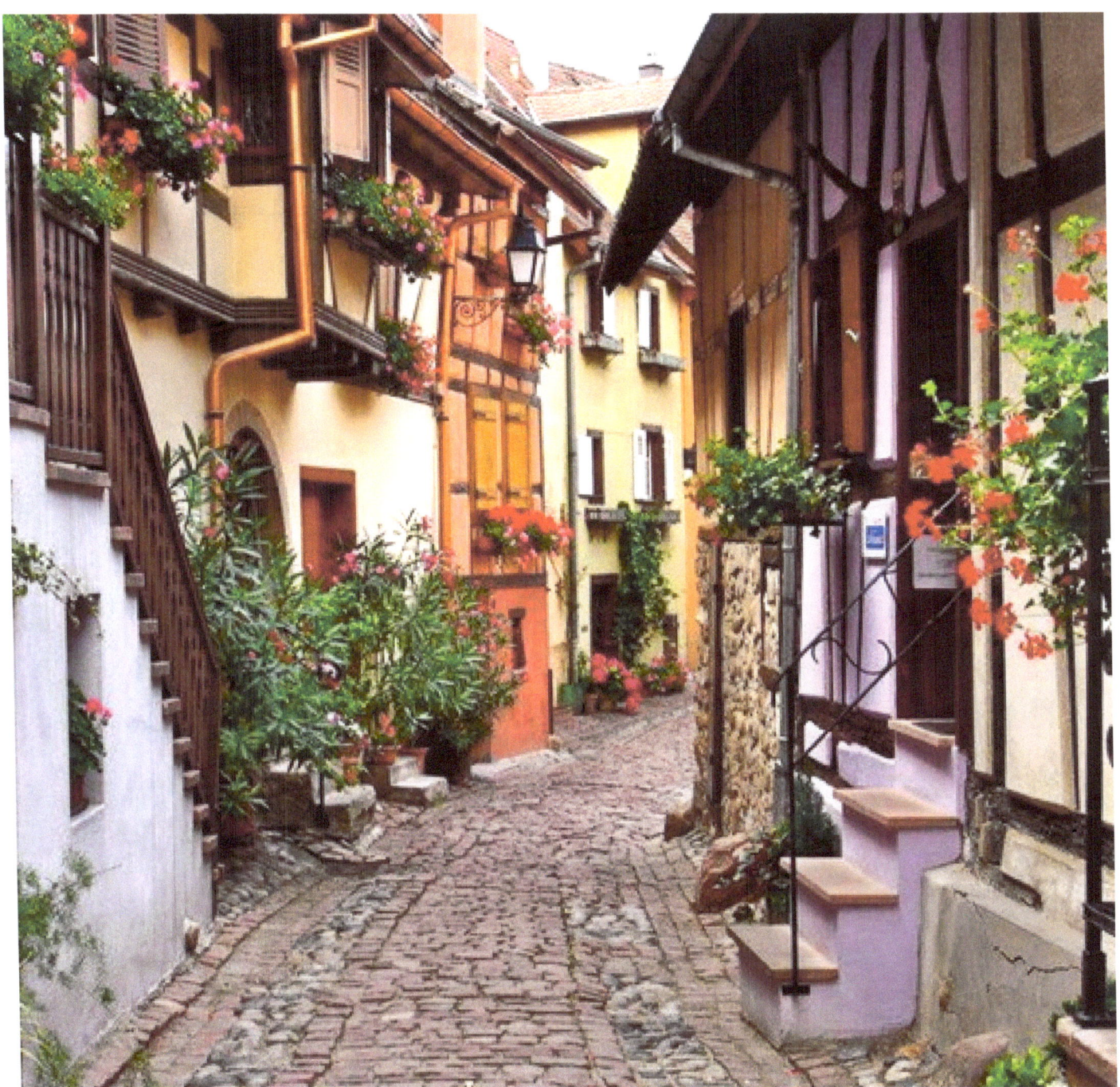

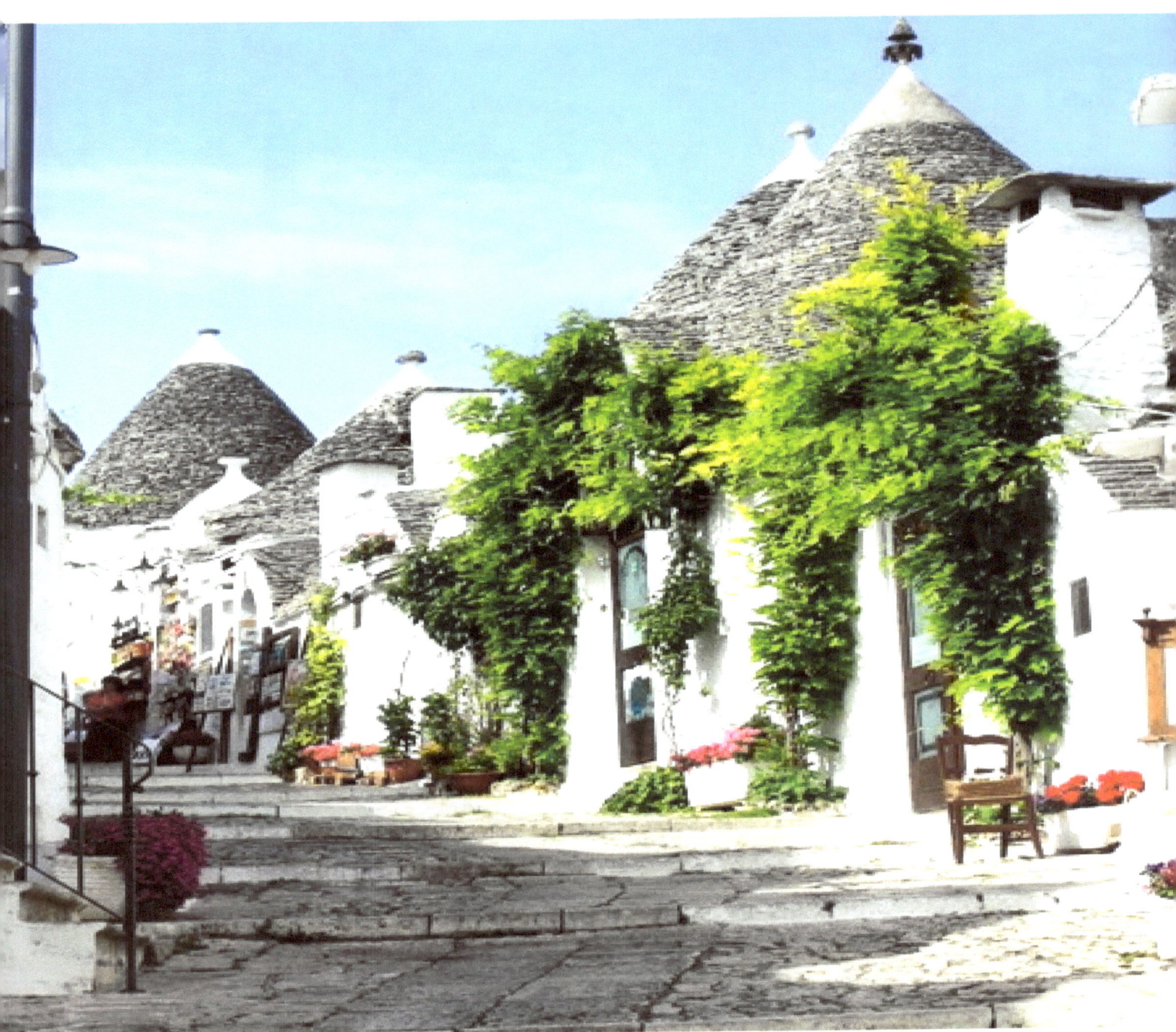

www.ingramcontent.com/pod-product-compliance
Lightning Source LLC
Chambersburg PA
CBHW050753180526
45159CB00003B/1446